NO GALLBLADDER DIET COOKBOOK

D1712496

150+ Mouthwatering Recipes | Ultimate Diet Guide for Health and Wellness after Gallbladder Removal Surgery | Pain Relief Cookbook for Gallbladder Disorder

Valerie Estrada

INTRODUCTION

Gallstones (cholelithiasis, improperly known as "liver stones") represent a very common disease, present in 10-15% of the population and more common in women around forty years old. The stones are formed inside the gallbladder, an organ located under the liver, on the right side of the abdomen, used to collect bile, the liquid produced by the liver that allows the digestion of fats. This liquid is composed of cholesterol, fats and bilirubin, elements that can be in excess and cause the crystallization of bile, thus forming solid compounds similar to pebbles, which can be only a few millimeters to several centimeters large. Gallstones can obstruct the passage of bile and cause very painful symptoms by inflaming the gallbladder, bile ducts and liver, with serious consequences over time.

Obesity and overweight, a diet too rich in fat and low in fiber, type II diabetes, constipation, but also rapid weight loss due to low-calorie diets can predispose the body to the formation of gallstones.

Symptoms and diagnosis of cholelithiasis

Many people who suffer from cholelithiasis remain without symptoms for many years and may never develop any. In other cases, however, the stones may cause symptoms or even severe complications (e.g., acute cholecystitis, gallbladder empyema, angiocolitis, acute pancreatitis).
The most common symptom referable with certainty to gallstones is biliary colic (also improperly called "liver colic"), which often occurs after a meal and causes:
sudden, sharp pain felt on the right side of the abdomen or near the sternum (sub-sternal), often in the form of twinges that can last from a few tens of minutes to several hours;
nausea and vomiting ;
fever or chills
back pain ;
attacks of diarrhea , with soft, clear stools (hypopigmented);
yellow skin and eyes (jaundice and subictus).
To diagnose cholelithiasis it is necessary to undergo an abdominal ultrasound . Treatment is necessary if you have chronic symptoms or if there is a current or probable risk of complications and can be pharmacological (drugs that are able to dissolve the stones) or, in severe cases, surgical (removal of the gallbladder). In any case, it is a good idea for the doctor to define the symptoms very carefully before attributing them with certainty to gallstones.

GENERAL DIETARY RECOMMENDATIONS

Observing a correct and balanced diet helps to prevent the formation of stones or, if already present and symptomatic, to reduce the episodes of gallstones and to improve the effectiveness of drugs for the treatment of the disease. It is therefore necessary to:

Consume small, well-divided meals throughout the day to improve gallbladder motility and reduce the risk of cholesterol accumulation in the bile (oversaturation).

Maintain good daily hydration (at least 2 L of water per day).

Prefer simple preparations, such as steaming, grilling, grilled, baked or baked in foil.

Avoid an unbalanced diet, especially if too rich in fat.

Increase consumption of fruits and vegetables and reduce consumption of sweets and sugary drinks.

Give preference to whole foods, such as bread and pasta, as they reduce the absorption of cholesterol.

Consume foods that help regularize gastric and intestinal transit (see following chapters).

The three chapters that follow indicate the foods to avoid, to limit and those generally advisable in the presence of the disease, but not the frequency or the quantity necessary for a balanced diet, which can and must be prescribed only by the medical specialist.

FOODS NOT ALLOWED

- Spirits and alcohol, including wine and beer.
- Fatty condiments such as butter, bacon, lard, cream, margarine, etc.
- Sauces with cream, very cooked sauces with large amounts of oil (e.g. Bolognese sauce).
- Mayonnaise, ketchup, mustard, bbq and other elaborate sauces.
- Meat broth, broth extracts, meat extracts and ready-made soups containing such ingredients.
- Sausages high in saturated fat such as bologna, salami, sausage, bacon, coppa, cracklings, cotechino, pig's trotter, etc.
- Fatty fish (e.g., eel, herring, salmon, eel, etc.), mollusks and crustaceans (e.g., octopus, cuttlefish, squid, mussels, clams, shrimp and prawns, langoustines, lobster, etc.).
- Fatty, smoked, marinated and salted meats. Game and offal.
- Visible fat of meats and cold cuts.
- Spicy and fermented cheeses.
- Whole milk.
- Typical fast food or junk food (eg: bacon and french fries, fried chicken nuggets, fried melted cheese nuggets, chips and pre-packaged snacks, etc.) because in these foods there can be high concentrations of trans fats formed during cooking (crispy or fried with exceeding the smoke point, rancidity, etc.) that, if taken in excess, are harmful to health. These fats (trans fats) can also be present in many products prepared industrially, artisanally and in ready made dishes, therefore it is always advisable to read nutritional labels and avoid foods whose ingredients include the words "hydrogenated vegetable fats".
- Sweets such as cakes, pastries, ice cream, puddings, etc., especially those filled with elaborated creams.
- Sugary drinks such as tonic water, cola, orangeade, iced teas, but also fruit juices, as they naturally contain sugar (fructose) even if the package says "no added sugar".

FOODS ALLOWED WITH MODERATION

- Salt should be reduced when added to food during and after cooking and limit the consumption of foods that naturally contain high quantities of salt (e.g. canned or pickled foods, meat cubes and extracts, soy sauces).
- Eggs.
- Vegetable oils rich in polyunsaturated or monounsaturated fatty acids, such as extra virgin olive oil, rice oil or single-seed oils (e.g. soybean, sunflower, corn, peanut), to be dosed with a teaspoon to control the amount.
- Dry oleaginous nuts, such as walnuts, hazelnuts, almonds, peanuts, cashews, etc..

PERMITTED AND RECOMMENDED FOODS

- Bread, pasta, rice, polenta, barley, spelt, potatoes (complex carbohydrates in general), but also rusks, breakfast cereals and dry cookies. Encourage the consumption of whole foods because fiber helps reduce the absorption of cholesterol, to alternate with foods prepared with white flour (50/50 ratio).
- Ripe fruits and vegetables in season, often changing colors to promote a proper intake of vitamins, minerals and antioxidants. Consume at least two portions of fruit and three of vegetables per day.
- Meat (both red and white) from lean cuts and without visible fat. Poultry should be eaten without the skin, as it is the part that provides the most fat.
- Lean sliced meats such as sweet raw ham, cooked ham and speck (without visible fat), bresaola, sliced turkey or chicken, to be consumed once or twice a week.
- Fresh lean fish (e.g. hake, sole, sea bass, dogfish, etc.).
- Semi-skimmed or skimmed milk and yogurt.
- Fresh low-fat cheese (for example milk flakes, primo sale, ricotta cheese, caciottina, crescenza, etc.) or aged cheese but with lower quantities of fats such as Grana Padano DOP, which is partially skimmed during the production process and therefore contains less lipids than the whole milk used to produce it. A 50g portion of Grana Padano DOP can be consumed 2/3 times a week in substitution of a second course of meat or eggs or it can also be used grated every day (a spoonful of 10g) in order to add flavor to dishes instead of salt. The consumption of Grana Padano PDO increases the protein intake at meals (high biological value proteins with 9 essential amino acids) and helps to achieve the daily requirement of calcium.
- Water, drink at least 2 liters per day, to be distributed equally throughout the day. You can also drink unsweetened herbal teas or infusions.
- Practical advice
- In case of overweight or obesity it is recommended to lose weight, to regularize the abdominal circumference (waist circumference values higher than 94 cm in men and 80 cm in women are associated with a "moderate" cardiovascular risk; values higher than 102 cm in men and 88 cm in women are associated with a "high" cardiovascular risk) and the fat mass, which you can easily measure for free with this tool. To eliminate the excess pounds you can subscribe to this weight control program

completely free of charge, which provides many tasty menus of the Italian tradition tailored to your daily caloric needs. If you are vegetarian, you can sign up for this other free program that, in addition to helping you lose weight, respects the environment and animals. Remember that returning to a normal weight allows you to reduce the risk of developing gallstones, as well as cardiovascular risk factors (high blood pressure, hypercholesterolemia, hypertriglyceridemia, insulin resistance).

- Avoid do-it-yourself diets: an excessively sudden weight loss can lead to the appearance of gallstones. In addition, a diet too low in calories can reduce lean mass (muscles) with the risk of reducing the effectiveness of the metabolism and recovering the weight lost with interest (yo-yo effect).
- Make the lifestyle more active, practice physical activity at least three times a week (minimum 150 minutes per week, optimal 300 minutes). Choose activities with aerobic characteristics (moderate intensity and long duration), such as cycling, aerobic gymnastics, walking at 4 km / h, low-intensity swimming, etc., as they are more effective in eliminating excess fat and prevent cholelithiasis.
- Do not smoke !

Warnings

All recommendations and advice in this article are for educational and informational purposes only and refer to the subject matter in general, therefore they cannot be considered as advice or prescriptions suitable for the individual, whose clinical picture and health conditions may require a different diet. The above mentioned information, recommendations and advices are not meant to be a medical or dietary prescription, therefore the reader must not, in any way, consider them as a substitute for the prescriptions or advices given by his or her own doctor.

Breakfast

---

1. Pineapple Smoothie

Tot time: 5 Minutes

Preparation time: 5 Minutes

Cooking Time: N/A

Servings: 1

What you need:

- ½ cup fresh or drained canned pineapple
- ⅛ cup orange juice
- ¼ cup plain yogurt
- ⅛ cup water
- 2 ice cubes, crushed

Steps:

1. Mix pineapple, orange juice, plain yogurt, water, and ice cubes in a mixer.
2. Cover and mix until smooth.

Per serving:

Calories: 99; Total Fat: 0.9g; Cholesterol: 4mg; Sodium: 44mg; Total Carbohydrate: 18.4g; Dietary Fiber: 1.2g; Total Sugars: 15g; Protein: 4.1g

---

2. Healthy Millet Porridge with Toasted Nut & Seeds

Tot time: 40 Minutes

Preparation time: 10 Minutes

Cooking Time: 30 Minutes

Makes: 2

What you need:

- 2 cups unsweetened almond milk
- ½ cup hulled millet
- 2 tablespoons chopped walnuts
- 2 tablespoons slivered almonds
- 2 tablespoons shredded unsweetened coconut
- 1 tablespoon flax seeds

- 2 tablespoons pumpkin seeds
- ¼ teaspoon ground nutmeg
- ½ teaspoon ground cinnamon

Steps:

1. Grind millet in a food processor; set aside.
2. Toast almonds and walnuts in a nonstick skillet over medium-high heat for about 5 minutes or until golden brown. Stir in flaxseeds, pumpkin seeds, and coconut, toast for 5 minutes more, and then remove from heat.
3. Add millet to the skillet and toast for about 3 minutes or until fragrant. Stir in 1 ½ cups of almond milk and bring to a gentle boil; lower heat and simmer for about 10 minutes. Stir in half of the toasted seed mixture, cinnamon, and nutmeg and simmer for another 10 minutes.
4. Serve the porridge in two bowls and top with the remaining almond milk and toasted seed mixture.

Per serving:

Calories: 397; Total Fat: 14.6 g; Net Carbs: 31.7 g; Dietary Fiber: 8.7 g; Sugars: 0.9; Protein: 12.6 g; Cholesterol: 0 mg; Sodium: 186 mg

---

3. Chili Avocado & Mashed Peas Breakfast Toast

Tot time: 15 Minutes

Preparation time: 5 Minutes

Cooking Time: 10 Minutes

Makes: 4

What you need:

- 4 slices of whole-wheat toast
- 2 avocados
- 2 cups frozen peas
- 1 tablespoon coconut oil
- 2 tablespoons mixed seeds
- 1 teaspoon chili oil
- A pinch of sea salt
- A pinch of black pepper

Steps:

1. Toast seeds in a pan for about 5 minutes or until golden.
2. Heat butter in a separate pan and then add in peas; cook for about 5 minutes and then remove from heat.
3. Mash the peas with a hand mixer until smooth; season with salt and pepper.

4. Butter your toast and top each with sliced avocado, mashed peas, and toasted mixed seeds; drizzle with chili oil and serve right away.

Per serving:

Calories: 445; Total Fat: 30.3 g; Net Carbs: 17.4 g; Dietary Fiber: 15.9 g; Sugars: 6; Protein: 13.9 g; Cholesterol: 0 mg; Sodium: 318 mg

---

4. Spiced Omelet with Red Onions & Chili

Tot time: 20 Minutes

Preparation time: 10 Minutes

Cooking Time: 10 Minutes

Makes: 2

What you need:

- 2 tablespoons olive oil
- 2 red onions, chopped
- 1 green chili, chopped
- 1 small tomato, chopped
- 3 eggs
- 1 teaspoon lemon juice
- ½ teaspoon turmeric powder
- ½ teaspoon red chili powder
- 2 tablespoons coriander, chopped
- Salt to taste

Steps:

1. In a bowl, mix chili, coriander, green chilies, chopped onions, and turmeric powder until well mixed; whisk in the eggs and season with salt and pepper.
2. In a skillet, heat oil and then pour in about a third of the mixture; swirl the pan to spread the egg mixture and cook for about 1 minute per side or until the egg is set. Transfer to a plate and keep warm. Repeat with the remaining mixture. Serve hot with chili sauce and a glass of fresh orange juice or chai for a satisfying breakfast.

Nutritional Info per **Makes:**

Calories: 241; Total Fat: 20.4 g; Carbs: 6.2 g; Dietary Fiber: 1.6 g; Sugars: 3.3 g; Protein: 9.2 g; Cholesterol: 246 mg; Sodium: 174 mg

---

5. Antioxidant-Rich Coconut & Blackberry Smoothie Bowl

Tot time: 5 Minutes

Preparation time: 5 Minutes

Cooking Time: N/A

Makes: 4

Ingredients

- 2 cups fresh blackberries
- 2 cups fresh spinach
- 1 cup coconut milk
- 1 ripe banana
- 2 tablespoons raw pumpkin seeds
- 2 tablespoons chia seeds
- ½ cup coconut flakes, toasted

Directions

1. In a mixer, mix almond milk, banana, and spinach until very smooth and creamy; add blackberries and pulse to mix well. Divide the smooth among serving bowls and top each serving with fresh blackberries, pumpkin seeds, chia seeds, and toasted coconut flakes.
2. Have a healthy meal!

Per serving:

Calories: 272; Total Fat: 20.7 g; Carbs: 22.2 g; Dietary Fiber: 9.6 g; Sugars: 9.8 g; Protein: 4.8 g; Cholesterol: 0 mg; Sodium: 25 mg

Calories: 70; Total Fat: 0.9g; Cholesterol: 1mg; Sodium: 11mg; Total Carbohydrate: 13.7g; Dietary Fiber: 2.4g;

6. Banana Protein Smoothie

Tot time: 5 Minutes

Preparation time: 5 Minutes

Cooking Time: N/A

Servings: 4

What you need:

- 1 banana, frozen
- 1 scoop vanilla protein powder
- ½ cup coconut milk
- 2 tsp unsweetened cocoa powder
- 1 tsp honey (optional)

Steps:

1. Mix banana, milk, vanilla protein powder, cocoa powder, and honey in a mixer.
2. Cover and mix until smooth.

Per serving:

Calories: 307; Total Fat: 3.5g; Cholesterol: 12mg; Sodium: 113mg; Total Carbohydrate: 41.2g; Dietary Fiber: 4.8g; Total Sugars: 26g; Protein: 33g

---

7. Banana Cauliflower Smoothie

Tot time: 5 Minutes

Preparation time: 5 Minutes

Cooking Time: N/A

Servings: 1

What you need:

- ½ cup frozen riced cauliflower
- ¼ cup frozen mixed berries
- ½ cup sliced frozen banana
- 1 cup unsweetened coconut milk
- 1 tsp honey (optional)

Steps:

1. Mix riced cauliflower, mixed berries, banana, coconut milk, and honey in a mixer.
2. Cover and mix until smooth.

Per serving:

Calories 168 Total Fat 4.4g 6% Saturated Fat 4.1g 20% Cholesterol 0mg 0% Sodium 49mg 2% Total Carbohydrate 31.7g 12% Dietary Fiber 5.2g 19% Total Sugars 18.4g Protein 2.1g

---

8. Wholesome Buckwheat Pancakes

Tot time: 20 Minutes

Preparation time: 10 Minutes

Cooking Time: 10 Minutes

Makes: 2

What you need:

- ⅔ cup raw buckwheat groats, soaked overnight and rinsed
- 1 egg
- ¼ teaspoon cinnamon
- 1 teaspoon stevia
- ¼ teaspoon sea salt
- ½ cup water

Steps:

1. Transfer rinsed and drained buckwheat to a mixer and add in egg, stevia, cinnamon, salt, and water and mix until very smooth.
2. Grease a nonstick skillet and set over medium heat; pour in about a third cup of the buckwheat batter, spreading to cover the bottom of the skillet. Cook for about 2 minutes over the side or until the pancake is golden brown. Repeat with the remaining batter.
3. Serve right away with a glass of orange juice.

Per serving:

Calories: 166; Total Fat: 3.5 g; Net Carbs: 26.4 g; Dietary Fiber: 4.2 g; Sugars: 1.2 g; Protein: 7.8 g; Cholesterol: 82 mg; Sodium: 271 mg

---

9. Healthy Sweet Potato & Turkey Breakfast Casserole

Tot time: 50 Minutes

Preparation time: 5 Minutes

Cooking Time: 45 Minutes

Makes: 6

What you need:

- 1 tablespoon coconut oil
- 1/2-pound ground turkey
- 1 large sweet potato, cut into slices
- 1/2 cup spinach
- 12 eggs
- Salt and pepper

Steps:

1. Preheat oven to 350°F. Lightly coat a square baking tray with coconut oil and set it aside.
2. In a skillet set over medium heat, brown ground turkey in coconut oil; season well and remove from heat.

3. Layer the potato slices onto the baking tray and top with raw spinach and ground turkey.
4. In a small bowl, whisk the salt, eggs, and pepper until thoroughly mixd; pour over the mixture to completely cover; bake for 45 minutes, or until the eggs are cooked through and the potatoes are soft. Now remove from the oven and let it set aside to cool slightly before serving.

Per serving:

Calories: 247; Total Fat: 15.2 g; Net Carbs: 5.9 g; Dietary Fiber: 1.1 g; Sugars: 2.6; Protein: 22.1 g; Cholesterol: 366 mg; Sodium: 176 mg

---

10. Healthy Coconut Yogurt with Acai Berry Granola

Tot time: 5 Minutes

Preparation time: 5 Minutes

Cook time: N/A

Makes: 2

What you need:

- 2 cup unflavored coconut yogurt
- 2 teaspoons raw honey
- ½ cup granola cereal
- ½ cup frozen acai berries

Steps:

1. Pour the yogurt in a serving bowl or a glass, stir in raw honey, top with granola, and sprinkle acai berries on top.
2. Have a healthy meal!

Per serving:

Calories: 230 Total Fat: 18.2 g; Carbs: 45.5 g; Dietary Fiber: 5.5 g; Sugars: 2.2 g; Protein: 29.1 g; Cholesterol: 20mg; Sodium: 120 mg

---

11. Avgolemono

Tot time: 30 Minutes

Preparation time: 10 Minutes

Cooking Time: 20 Minutes

Makes: 4

What you need:

- 2cups cooked chicken, shredded using a fork
- 5 cups homemade chicken broth
- 1 egg
- 2 tablespoons freshly squeezed lemon juice
- 1 cup cooked squash, scooped out using a fork
- 3 tablespoons freshly chopped parsley
- Freshly ground pepper, to taste
- Kosher salt, to taste
- ¼ cup grated goat cheese

Steps:

1. Pour the chicken broth into a pot, then stir in the shredded chicken over high heat. Once it begins to boil, reduce the heat to low and continue to cook for 5 minutes before setting aside. Whisk the egg and lemon juice in a large bowl until frothy.
2. Slowly pour in two cups of the broth mixture as you continue until perfectly mixed, then pour this into the chicken broth pot. Stir in shredded squash into the pot, heat it for about 5-10 minutes, and season with salt and pepper. Turn off heat and stir in the grated cheese and chopped parsley.
3. Add chopped parsley and cheese, and serve hot!

Per serving:

Calories: 289; Total Fat: 15 g; Net Carbs: 4 g; Dietary Fiber: 6.2 g; Sugars: 1.9; Protein: 33 g; Cholesterol: 0 mg; Sodium: 205 mg

---

12. Cheesy Pancakes

Tot time: 35 Minutes

Preparation time: 15 Minutes

Cooking Time: 20 Minutes

Makes: 10

What you need:

- 1 cup ricotta cheese
- 2 teaspoons baking powder
- 1cup instant oats
- 1 cup egg whites
- 1 tablespoon maple syrup
- ½ teaspoon pure vanilla extract
- Pinch of salt

- Berries for serving, optional

Steps:

1. In a mixer, finely mix the oats. Mix in the egg whites and cheese, add the baking powder and maple syrup, and continue mixing until mixed. Add in vanilla extract and mix to incorporate. Place a nonstick pan on medium to low heat and use a spoon to add the butter to the pan or a griddle.
2. Cook for 4 minutes or until bubbles form, flip and cook the remaining side for 2 minutes. Continue cooking until all the batter is done.
3. Serve with berries and maple syrup.
4. Have a healthy meal!

Per serving:

Calories: 431; Total Fat: 65 g; Net Carbs: 12 g; Dietary Fiber: 6g; Sugars: 5; Protein: 26 g; Cholesterol: 512 mg; Sodium: 565 mg

---

13. Blueberry Smoothie

Tot time: 10 Minutes

Preparation time: 10 Minutes

Cooking Time: 0 Minutes

Makes: 2

What you need:

- ½ cup frozen blueberries
- 1 cup unsweetened almond milk
- 1 tablespoon almond butter
- ¼ cup ice cubes
- 1 pinch of salt

Steps:

1. First in a mixer, mix all of the ingredients and mix until smooth.
2. Serve right away.
3. Have a healthy meal!

Per serving:

Calories: 221; Total Fat: 35 g; Net Carbs: 27 g; Dietary Fiber: 2g; Sugars: 4.1; Protein: 24 g; Cholesterol: 0 mg; Sodium: 191 mg

14. Healthy Buckwheat, Millet, and Amaranth Porridge with Toasted Hazelnuts

Tot time: 40 Minutes

Preparation time: 10 Minutes

Cooking Time: 30 Minutes

Makes: 4

What you need:

- 1/2 cup buckwheat groats
- 1/2 cup whole-grain amaranth
- 1/2 cup whole grain millet
- 5 cups water
- 1 teaspoon kosher salt
- 1 tablespoon flax seeds
- 2 cups almond milk
- 1 teaspoon ground cinnamon
- 1/8 teaspoon ground nutmeg
- 2 tablespoons raw honey
- 4 tablespoons toasted hazelnuts, coarsely chopped

Directions

1. Rinse the grains and add to a pot of boiling salted water; lower heat and simmer for about 30 minutes or until the grains are cooked through.
2. Remove from heat and stir in almond milk; divide among serving bowl, drizzle each serving with raw honey, and sprinkle with cinnamon and nutmeg. Top with toasted hazelnuts and Have a healthy meal!

Per serving:

Calories: 318; Total Fat: 7.4 g; Carbs: 55.7 g; Dietary Fiber: 7.3 g; Sugars: 9.3 g; Protein: 9.5 g; Cholesterol: 0 mg; Sodium: 644 mg

15. Avocado Spirulina Chia Pudding with Toasted Coconut & Blueberries

Tot time: 35 Minutes

Preparation time: 10 Minutes

Cooking Time: N/A

Servings: 4

What you need:

- 5 tablespoons chia seeds
- 1/2 cup coconut milk
- 1 cup almond milk
- 2 teaspoons organic raw honey
- 1 teaspoon spirulina powder
- 1 avocado, diced
- 1 ripe banana
- 1 tablespoon chia seeds to serve
- A handful of fresh blueberries to serve
- 2 tablespoons toasted coconut flakes

Steps:

1. In a bowl, mix together coconut milk, almond milk, raw honey, and chia seeds; let sit for at least 30 min or until all liquid is absorbed. In a food processor, mix together spirulina, banana, and avocado until very smooth. Divide the chia seed mixture into serving bowls and top each serving with a layer of spirulina puree. Serve topped with toasted coconut flakes, chia seeds, and fresh blueberries.

Per serving:

Calories: 419; Total Fat: 31.1 g; Carbs: 23.3 g; Dietary Fiber: 16.6 g; Sugars: 10.2 g; Protein: 8.6 g; Cholesterol: 0 mg; Sodium: 23 mg

---

16. Mango Ginger Smoothie

Tot time: 5 Minutes

Preparation time: 5 Minutes

Cooking Time: N/A

Servings: 2

What you need:

- 1 cup cooked lentils cooled
- 2 cups frozen mango chunks
- 1-½ cups orange juice
- 2 tsp chopped fresh ginger
- 2 tsp maple syrup (optional)
- Pinch of ground nutmeg, plus more for garnish
- 6 ice cubes

Steps:

1. Put the lentils, mango, orange juice, ginger, maple syrup, nutmeg, and ice cubes in a mixer.
2. Beat over high heat for 2 to 3 minutes until smooth.
3. Garnish with more nutmeg if desired.

Per serving:

Calories: 292; Total Fat: 1.4g; Cholesterol: 0mg; Sodium: 239mg; Total Carbohydrate: 62.8g; Dietary Fiber: 11g; Total Sugars: 38.8g; Protein: 11.3g

---

17. Kiwi Strawberry Banana Smoothie

Tot time: 5 Minutes

Preparation time: 5 Minutes

Cooking Time: N/A

Servings: 4

What you need:

- 2 cups sliced fresh strawberries
- 1 small banana, sliced
- ½ (6 ounces) container low-fat Greek yogurt
- 1 cup ice cubes
- ½ kiwi fruit, peeled and sliced

Steps:

1. In a mixer, mix all ingredients.
2. Cover and mix until smooth.

Per serving:

---

18. Healthy Spiced Turmeric Cassava Pancakes

Tot time: 20 Minutes

Preparation time: 10 Minutes

Cooking Time: 10 Minutes

Makes: 4

What you need:

- 3/4 cup cassava flour
- 1/2 cup coconut milk

- 2 free-range eggs
- 1/4 cup coconut oil, melted
- 1/2 teaspoon baking soda
- 1 teaspoon stevia
- 1 teaspoon ground ginger
- 1 teaspoon ground turmeric
- 1 teaspoon ground cinnamon
- 1/2 teaspoon ground black pepper
- 1/2 tablespoon toasted coconut flakes
- 1 tablespoon macadamia nut butter
- 1 tablespoon melted coconut butter

Directions

1. Mix all dry ingredients in a large bowl. In another bowl, whisk the eggs and stir in coconut milk and coconut oil until well mixed.
2. Now add to the dry ingredients and whisk to form a smooth batter.
3. Heat a tablespoon of coconut oil in a medium skillet and cook in two spoonfuls of the batter for about 2 minutes; flip to cook the other side until golden brown. Repeat with the remaining batter. Serve topped with macadamia butter, coconut butter, and coconut flakes. Have a healthy meal!

Per serving:

Calories: 314 Total Fat: 28.1 g; Carbs: 20.5 g; Dietary Fiber: 3.5 g; Sugars: 1.1 g; Protein: 4.1 g; Cholesterol: 87 mg; Sodium: 228 mg

---

19. Superfood Overnight Oats

Tot time: 10 Minutes + Chilling Time

Preparation time: 10 Minutes

Cooking Time: N/A

Makes: 2

What you need:

- 1/2 cup old-fashioned oats
- 1 teaspoon chia seeds
- 1/2 cup vanilla almond milk (unsweetened)
- 1/4 cup fresh blueberries
- 1/4 banana, chopped
- 1/4 cup chopped fresh pineapple
- 1/4 cup nonfat Greek yogurt
- 1/4 teaspoon cinnamon

- 1 tablespoon chopped toasted almonds

Directions

1. In a small container, mix oats, chia seeds, almond milk, blueberries, banana, pineapple, yogurt, cinnamon, and chopped toasted almonds. Refrigerate for 24 hours.
2. Remove from the refrigerator and whisk thoroughly before serving.

Per serving:

Calories: 310; Total Fat: 18.4 g; Dietary Fiber: 5 g; Carbs: 29 g; Protein: 10.8 g; Cholesterol: 3 mg; Sodium: 29 mg; Sugars: 10.2 g

20. Breakfast Amaranth with Toasted Walnuts

Tot time: 30 Minutes

Preparation time: 5 Minutes

Cooking Time: 25 Minutes

Makes: 6

What you need:

- 2 cups amaranth
- 4 cups water
- 1/2 teaspoon salt
- 1 cup chopped toasted walnuts

Directions

1. In a pan, mix amaranth, salt, and water and bring to a boil; cover and simmer for about 25 minutes or until liquid is absorbed; remove from heat and let cool for about 5 minutes.
2. Serve the amaranth topped with toasted walnuts.

Per serving:

Calories: 311; Total Fat: 15.5 g; Net Carbs: 29.3 g; Dietary Fiber: 6 g; Sugars: 1.1 g; Protein: 12.1 g; Cholesterol: 0 mg; Sodium: 209 mg

21. Spiced Hummus Avocado Toast

Tot time: 5 Minutes

Preparation time: 5 Minutes

Cooking Time: N/A

Makes: 1

What you need:

- 1 slice toasted whole wheat bread
- 2 tablespoons hummus
- 1/4 ripe avocado, sliced
- A pinch of red pepper flakes
- A pinch of sea salt
- A pinch of black pepper

Steps:

1. Spread the whole-wheat toast with hummus and top with avocado; sprinkle with red pepper flakes, sea salt, and pepper and serve right away.

Per serving:

Calories: 219; Total Fat: 15.5 g; Net Carbs: 13.1 g; Dietary Fiber: 7 g; Sugars: 1.8 g; Protein: 6.8 g; Cholesterol: 0 mg; Sodium: 475 mg

---

22. Nutty Superfood Grain-Free, Gluten-Free Breakfast Muesli

Tot time: 5 Minutes

Preparation time: 5 Minutes

Cooking Time: N/A

Makes: 6

What you need:

- 3 cups almond milk (or cashew milk)
- 1 cup hemp seeds
- 1/2 cup chia seeds
- 1 cup sunflower seeds
- 1 cup pumpkin seeds
- 1/4 cup dried apricot
- 1/4 cup dried cranberries
- 1/2 cup unsweetened toasted coconut flakes
- 1/4 cup fresh strawberries
- 1/4 cup fresh blueberries
- 1/4 cup fresh raspberries
- 1 apple, diced

Steps:

1. Mix seeds, dry fruit, and toasted coconut flakes in a large bowl; stir in milk until well mixd and then serve topped with berries and diced apple.

Per serving:

Calories: 471; Total Fat: 34.5 g; Carbs: 27.2 g; Dietary Fiber: 11 g; Sugars: 7.1 g; Protein: 17.9 g; Cholesterol: 0 mg; Sodium: 114 mg

---

23. Healthy Amaranth Porridge

Tot time: 40 Minutes

Preparation time: 10 Minutes

Cooking Time: 30 Minutes

Makes: 2

What you need:

- ½ cup amaranth
- 1 ½ cups water
- ¼ cup almond milk
- 1 teaspoon stevia
- ¼ teaspoon sea salt

Steps:

1. In a pan, mix water, salt, and amaranth and bring to a boil; cover and simmer for about 30 minutes and then stir in milk and stevia and cook, stirring until the porridge is creamy. Serve right away.

Per serving:

Calories: 190; Total Fat: 3.8 g; Net Carbs: 27.7 g; Dietary Fiber: 4.8 g; Sugars: 0.8 g; Protein: 7.3 g; Cholesterol: 0 mg; Sodium: 287 mg

---

24. Delicious Avocado Pancakes

Tot time: 20 Minutes

Preparation time: 10 Minutes

Cooking Time: 10 Minutes

Makes: 4

What you need:

- 1 ripe avocado

- 1 1/4 cups gluten-free oat flour
- 2 tablespoons lemon juice
- 1/2 cup almond milk
- 1 tablespoon raw honey
- 1 tablespoon baking powder
- 1 teaspoon matcha powder
- 1 teaspoon vanilla extract
- Pinch of salt
- A handful of fresh blueberries to serve

Steps:

1. Mix all of the ingredients in a mixer until smooth.
2. Heat oil in a skillet over medium heat; add in batter and spread into a circle. Cook for about 2 minutes per side or until browned. Repeat with the remaining batter. Serve topped with coconut butter and fresh blueberries.
3. Have a healthy meal!

Per serving:

Calories: 284; Total Fat: 13.3 g; Carbs: 34.8 g; Dietary Fiber: 7.6 g; Sugars: 2.7 g; Protein: 8.2 g; Cholesterol: 0 mg; Sodium: 69 mg

---

25. Gluten-Free Nut Breakfast Cereal

Tot time: 30 Minutes

Preparation time: 5 Minutes

Cooking Time: 25 Minutes

Makes: 12

What you need:
- 1/4 cup raw almond pieces
- 1/4 cup raw walnuts pieces
- 4 cups gluten-free oats
- 1 teaspoon cinnamon
- 1/3 cup coconut oil, melted
- 1/3 cup raw honey
- ½ cup dried fruit (like raisins) to serve
- 1 cup almond milk, to serve

Steps:

1. Preheat the oven to 325 °F. In a large bowl, mix all of the dry ingredients; in a small mixing dish, mix the coconut oil and honey and add to the dry ingredients. Mix until the oats are wet.

2. Place the mixture on a baking sheet and lined with parchment paper. Bake in the oven for about 25 minutes or until golden browned.
3. To serve, add in dried fruit and then stir in almond milk. Have a healthy meal!

Per serving:

Calories: 202 Total Fat: 10.1 g; Carbs: 27.2 g; Dietary Fiber: 3.1 g; Sugars: 8.3 g; Protein: 4.1 g; Cholesterol: 0 mg; Sodium: 11 mg

---

26. Detoxifying Tropical Fruit Smoothie Breakfast Bowls

Tot time: 10 Minutes

Preparation time: 10 Minutes

Cooking Time: N/A

Makes: 4

What you need:

- ¾ cup chopped fresh pineapple
- 1 medium banana, frozen
- 2 cups frozen mango, diced
- 2 cups fresh baby spinach
- 1/2 cup freshly squeezed lemon juice
- 1 cup coconut milk
- 2 tablespoons honey
- 1/4 cup unsweetened toasted coconut
- 8 teaspoons chia seeds
- 1/4 cup chopped macadamia nuts
- 1 cup chopped fresh pineapple

Steps:

1. In a mixer, mix together banana, mango, lemon juice, pineapple, spinach, coconut milk, and honey until smooth.
2. Divide the mixture among serving bowls; top each serving with toasted coconut, chia seeds, toasted macadamia, and diced pineapple.
3. Have a healthy meal!

Per serving:

Calories: 318; Total Fat: 16 g; Carbs: 47 g; Dietary Fiber: 8 g; Sugars: 32 g; Protein: 5 g; Cholesterol: 0 mg; Sodium: 27 mg

---

27. Healthy Hot Multi-Grains Bowl

Tot time: 15 Minutes

Preparation time: 5 Minutes

Cooking Time: 10 Minutes

Makes: 1

What you need:

- 2 tablespoons chopped dried apricot
- ¼ cup multigrain cereal
- 1 cup almond milk
- ¼ shredded carrot
- ¼ teaspoon ground cinnamon
- 1 teaspoon orange zest
- pinch salt
- pinch ground nutmeg
- 1 tablespoon toasted chopped almonds
- 1 orange, sliced
- 1 teaspoon raw honey

Steps:

1. Mix together cereal, half of the almond milk, apricot, carrot, cinnamon, orange zest, nutmeg, and salt in a saucepan; bring to a gentle boil and then stir to mix well.
2. Lower heat and simmer for about 8 minutes.
3. To serve, stir in the remaining almond milk and serve topped with toasted almonds, orange slices, and raw honey.

Per serving:

Calories: 285; Total Fat: 6 g; Carbs: 28.8 g; Dietary Fiber: 9 g; Sugars: 35 g; Protein: 7 g; Cholesterol: 0 mg; Sodium: 306 mg

---

28. Healthy Brown Rice Breakfast Bowl

Tot time: 20 Minutes

Preparation time: 10 Minutes

Cooking Time: 10 Minutes

Makes: 4

What you need:

- 2 cups cooked brown rice
- 1/2 cup unsweetened almond milk
- 1 teaspoon liquid stevia

- 1 tablespoon almond butter
- 1 apple, diced
- 2 dates, chopped
- 1/2 teaspoon cinnamon

Steps:

1. Mix almond oil, almond butter, stevia, apple, and dates in a saucepan; bring to a gentle boil and then cook for about 5 minutes or until the apples are tender; stir in cinnamon and brown rice and cook for about 5 minutes and then remove from heat.
2. Serve immediately.

Per serving:

Calories: 226; Total Fat: 4.3 g; Net Carbs: 34.4 g; Dietary Fiber: 4.8 g; Sugars: 8.6 g; Protein: 5.8 g; Cholesterol: 0 mg; Sodium: 26 mg

---

29. Buckwheat Cereal with Red Onions & Mushrooms

Tot time: 55 Minutes

Preparation time: 15 Minutes

Cooking Time: 40 Minutes

Makes: 4

What you need:

- 1 cup buckwheat groats
- 1 tablespoon olive oil, or to taste
- 1 red onion, diced
- 1 carrot, diced
- ½ pound mushrooms, diced
- 1 tablespoon butter
- 2 cups water
- A pinch of sea salt
- A pinch of black pepper

Steps:

1. Rinse buckwheat and drain.
2. Pre-heat a nonstick pan over medium heat and toast the buckwheat for about 5 minutes.
3. Place the mixture in a large mixing basin and set aside.
4. Now add olive oil to the skillet and cook in onions and carrots for about 10 minutes or until tender.
5. Stir in mushrooms and cook for about 5 minutes.

6. In a pot set over medium heat, melt butter and stir in buckwheat; add the onion mixture, salt, pepper, and water and bring a gentle boil. Simmer for about 20 minutes and then serve right away.

Per serving:

Calories: 185; Total Fat: 7.5 g; Net Carbs: 22.6 g; Dietary Fiber: 4.5 g; Sugars: 3.7 g Protein: 6 g; Cholesterol: 8 mg; Sodium: 101 mg

---

30. Coconut Buckwheat Pancakes

Tot time: 35 Minutes

Preparation time: 15 Minutes

Cooking Time: 20 Minutes

Makes: 5

What you need:

- 1 cup buckwheat groats
- 1 ½ cups boiling water
- 1 cup spelt flour
- ½ cup unsweetened shredded coconut
- 2 teaspoons baking powder
- 1 cup soy milk
- 1 egg
- 2 tablespoons oil
- 1 teaspoon liquid stevia
- 1 serving cooking spray

Steps:

1. Mix buckwheat and boiling water in a large bowl and sit for at least 10 minutes or until water is absorbed.
2. Heat a nonstick skillet over medium heat.
3. Whisk together buckwheat, coconut, flour, and baking powder in another bowl.
4. Whisk together oil, egg, milk, and liquid stevia; pour into the buckwheat mixture and wheat to mix well.
5. Grease a nonstick skillet and add about a third cup of the batter, spreading to cover the bottom. Cook for about 2 minutes per side or until the pancakes are golden browned.
6. Repeat with the remaining batter. Serve the pancakes with a glass of fresh orange juice.

Per serving:

Calories: 297; Total Fat: 11.7 g; Net Carbs: 36.8 g; Dietary Fiber: 6.1 g; Sugars: 6.8 g
Protein: 9.8 g; Cholesterol: 33 mg; Sodium: 69 mg

31. Passionfruit, Raspberry & Coconut Yoghurt Chia Parfait

Yield: 4 Servings

Tot time: 15 Minutes

Preparation time: 15 Minutes

Cooking Time: N/A

Makes: 4

What you need:

- 4 tablespoons organic chia seeds
- 2 cups almond milk
- ½ teaspoon raw honey
- ½ teaspoon natural vanilla extract
- 1 cup organic frozen raspberries
- 1/2 fresh banana
- 1/3 cup almond milk
- 1 tablespoon Lucuma powder
- 1 tablespoon raw honey
- 1 cup fresh passionfruit pulp
- 1 cup coconut yogurt

Steps:

1. Make the chia base by mixing milk, chia seeds, raw honey, and vanilla extract until well mixd; let rest for a few minutes.
2. In a mixer, mix together the frozen raspberries, almond milk, banana, lucuma powder, and raw honey until very smooth.
3. To assemble, divide the chia seeds base among the bottom of tall serving glasses; layer with coconut yogurt, passion fruit pulp, and top with raspberry smooth. Serve garnished with fresh fruit and toasted walnuts.

Per serving:

Calories: 377; Total Fat: 20.7 g; Carbs: 27.3 g; Dietary Fiber: 15.4 g; Sugars: 16.9 g;
Protein: 8.1 g; Cholesterol: 0 mg; Sodium: 18 mg

Snacks & Desserts

32. Buckwheat Strawberry Pancakes

Tot time: 30 Minutes

Preparation time: 10 Minutes

Cooking Time: 20 Minutes

Servings: 4

What you need:

- 2 egg whites
- 1 tbsp coconut oil
- ½ cup coconut milk
- ½ cup coconut flour
- ½ cup buckwheat flour
- ½ cup almond flour
- 1 tbsp baking powder
- 1 tbsp coconut sugar
- ½ cup sparkling water
- 3 cups sliced fresh strawberries

Steps:

1. Whisk together the coconut oil, egg whites, and coconut milk in a small bowl.
2. In another bowl, mix the flours, baking powder, and coconut sugar. Add sparkling water and egg, oil, and milk mixture and stir for a couple of minutes.
3. Place a non-stick frying pan over medium heat. When a drop of water sizzles as it hits the pan, spoon ½ cup pancake batter into the pan.
4. Bale a pancake for approx. 2 min on each side. The bottoms of the pancake should be brown and bubbly. Repeat with the remaining pancake batter.
5. Transfer the pancakes to individual plates. Top each with ½ cup sliced strawberries and serve immediately.

Per serving:

Calories: 143; Total Fat: 7.8g; Cholesterol: 0mg; Sodium: 21mg; Total Carbohydrate: 17.6g; Dietary Fiber: 3.4g; Total Sugars: 6.6g; Protein: 3.6g

33. Tangy Lime-Garlic Kale Shrimps

Tot time: 20 Minutes

Preparation time: 10 Minutes

Cooking Time: 10 Minutes

Servings: 4

What you need:

- 16 large shrimps - peeled, deveined, and tails on, or more to taste
- 3 cloves garlic (minced)
- 1 tsp of crushed red pepper
- 2 tsp seafood seasoning or to taste
- salt and ground black pepper to taste
- 2 tbsp lime juice
- 3 tbsp chopped fresh parsley
- 3 tsp lime zest
- 1 cup chopped kale

Steps:

1. Heat a large pan over medium-low heat for about 3 minutes. Add shrimps, garlic, and crushed red pepper all at once and stir.
2. Add seafood seasoning, salt, and black pepper. Mix everything together.
3. Cook over medium heat, approx. 5 minutes, until the shrimp are cooked through.
4. Add kale and cook for 2 min, then add the lime juice to the pot and stir again.
5. Reduce the heat to low. Add the parsley and lime zest. Transfer only the shrimps and kale to a serving dish.

Per serving:

Calories: 293; Total Fat: 3.2g; Cholesterol: 553mg; Sodium: 707mg; Total Carbohydrate: 3.3g; Dietary Fiber: 0.5g; Total Sugars: 0.5g; Protein: 59.7g

---

34. Apple Muffins with Cinnamon

Tot time: 35 Minutes

Prep time: 10 Minutes

Cook time: 25 Minutes

Servings: 16

What you need:

- 1 cup non-fat plain sour cream
- 2 eggs
- 2 tbsp coconut oil

- 2 tsp vanilla extract
- 1 cup almond flour
- 1 cup honey
- ¾ cup milled oats
- ¼ cup flaxseed meal
- 2 tsp cinnamon
- ¼ tsp nutmeg
- 1 ½ tsp baking powder
- ½ tsp salt
- 2 medium peeled and chopped apples

Steps:

1. Preheat oven to 350 Fand line the muffin pan with a liner or use a silicone muffin pan.
2. Mix sour cream, eggs, oil, and vanilla in a bowl.
3. Mix flour, oats, 1 cup honey, flax seeds, cinnamon, nutmeg, baking powder, and salt in a bowl. Turn on the mixer at low speed.
4. Add in the dry ingredients.
5. Stir until everything is well mixd. The dough should be lumpy. Work in the apples with a spatula.
6. Fill the muffin pan with about ¼ cup of batter into each muffin space.
7. Bake for about 22 minutes or until the top is golden and the toothpick comes out clean when you insert it.

Per serving:

Calories: 187; Total Fat: 3.9g; Cholesterol: 21mg; Sodium: 94mg; Total Carbohydrate: 29.4g; Dietary Fiber 3g; Total Sugars: 21.3g; Protein: 4.6g

---

35. Roasted Potatoes with Garlic and Parsley and Rosemary

Tot time: 35 Minutes

Prep time: 10 Minutes

Cook time: 25 Minutes

Servings: 4

What you need:

- ¾ pound small potatoes
- 4 garlic cloves
- 2 tsp coconut oil
- 2 tsp chopped fresh rosemary
- ⅛ tsp salt
- ¼ tsp ground black pepper

- 2 tsp butter
- 2 tbsp chopped fresh parsley

Steps:

1. Preheat oven to 400 F.
2. Lay a large baking dish with parchment paper.
3. Add the potatoes, garlic cloves, coconut oil, rosemary, salt, and pepper to a large bowl. Mix until the potatoes are coated with oil and spices.
4. Place the potatoes on the prepared baking dish, then cover and bake for 20-25 minutes.
5. Remove the lid or foil. Flip the potatoes and cook them, uncovered, until the potatoes are tender and lightly browned (about 25 minutes).
6. Put in a bowl and mix with butter. Sprinkle with parsley and serve.

Per serving:

Calories: 103; Total Fat: 4.4g; Cholesterol: 5mg; Sodium: 94mg; Total Carbohydrate: 15.1g; Dietary Fiber: 1.9g; Total Sugars: 0.9g; Protein 1.9g

---

36. Mixed Flour Banana Bread

Tot time: 1 Hour & 10 Minutes

Preparation time: 10 Minutes

Cooking Time: 60 Minutes

Servings: 14

What you need:

- ½ cup brown rice flour
- ½ cup amaranth flour
- ½ cup tapioca flour
- ½ cup millet flour
- ½ cup quinoa flour
- 1 tsp baking soda
- ½ tsp baking powder
- ⅛ tsp salt
- ¾ cup egg white
- 2 tbsp coconut oil
- ½ cup honey
- 2 cups mashed banana

Steps:

1. Preheat the oven to 350 F. Prepare a 5 x 9-inch loaf pan by spraying it lightly with cooking spray. Sprinkle with a little flour. Put aside.

2. Use a bowl to mix all dry ingredients (live out the sugar).
3. Mix the egg, oil, honey, and mashed banana in another bowl. Mix well.
4. Put the wet and dry mixtures together and stir until well mixd. Pour into a loaf pan. Bake for 50 to 60 minutes.
5. Take the bread out of the oven and let it cool for a bit.
6. Slice it and serve.

Per serving:

Calories: 152; Total Fat: 2.7g; Cholesterol: 0mg; Sodium: 114mg; Total Carbohydrate: 29.3g; Dietary Fiber: 2g; Total Sugars: 11.2g; Protein: 3.7g

---

37. Stuffed Mushrooms with Herbs

Tot time: 1 Hour & 10 Minutes

Preparation time: 10 Minutes

Cooking Time: 60 Minutes

Servings: 10

What you need:

- 10 mushrooms (without stems)

Topping:

- ¾ cup cornflakes (crushed)
- 2 tbsp melted coconut oil
- 1,5 tbsp fresh parsley

Filling:

- 1 cup fresh basil leaves
- 2 tbsp grated Parmesan cheese
- 1 tsp pine nuts
- 1 tsp pumpkin seed
- 1 tsp sunflower seeds
- 1 tsp olive oil
- 1 tsp minced garlic
- 1 tsp freshly squeezed lemon juice
- Pinch of salt

Steps:

1. Preheat oven to 350 F.
2. Line a baking sheet with baking paper. Place mushrooms on a baking sheet upside down.

3. Mix the crushed cornflakes, coconut oil, and chopped parsley in a small bowl for the topping. Set aside.
4. Place the basil, Parmesan, pumpkin seeds, sunflower seeds, pine nuts, olive oil, garlic, salt, and lemon juice in a food processor for the filling. Process until well mixd.
5. Fill the mushroom caps with the filling and sprinkle each mushroom with about 1 tsp of topping.
6. Bake for 10 or 15 minutes or until the mushrooms are golden brown.

Per serving:

Calories: 51; Total Fat: 2.9g; Cholesterol: 0mg; Sodium: 121mg; Total Carbohydrate: 5.4g; Dietary Fiber: 0.9g; Total Sugars: 0.5g; Protein: 1.5g

---

38. Chicken Tenders with Pineapple

Tot time: 30 Minutes

Preparation time: 20 min

Cooking Time: 10 min

Servings: 10

What you need:

- 1cup pineapple juice
- ½ cup honey
- ⅓ cup light soy sauce
- 2 pounds chicken breast strips
- skewers

Steps:

1. Mix the pineapple juice, honey, and soy sauce in a small saucepan over medium heat. Remove from heat just before cooking.
2. Place the chicken fillets in a medium bowl. Cover with the pineapple marinade and store in the refrigerator for at least 30 minutes.
   Preheat the grill to medium heat. Thread the chicken lengthwise onto wooden skewers.
3. Lightly grease the grill. Grill the chicken fillets for 5 minutes per side or until juices run clear.
4. They cook quickly, so watch them closely.

Per serving:

Calories: 99; Total Fat: 1g; Cholesterol: 7mg; Sodium: 300mg; Total Carbohydrate: 20.1g; Dietary Fiber: 0.1g; Total Sugars: 16.7g; Protein: 3.7g

39. Nutmeg Apple Frozen Yogurt

Tot time: 45 Minutes

Preparation time: 5 Minutes

Cooking Time: 40 Minutes

Servings: 4

What you need:

- 2 apples halves
- 1 cup Greek yogurt
- ½ cup coconut sugar
- ¼ tsp ground nutmeg
- ⅛ tsp ground cinnamon

Steps:

1. Puree the apple in a mixer.
2. Mix apple, Greek yogurt, coconut sugar, cinnamon, and nutmeg in an ice cream jar.
3. Freeze for two or more hours.

Per serving:

Calories: 91; Total Fat: 1.1g; Cholesterol: 3mg; Sodium: 21mg; Total Carbohydrate: 15.5g; Dietary Fiber: 2.6g; Total Sugars: 10.6g; Protein: 5.2g

40. Chocolate Cookies without Flour

Tot time: 20 Minutes

Preparation time: 5 Minutes

Cooking Time: 15 Minutes

Servings: 8

What you need:

- ½ cup powdered sugar
- 1 tsp corn-starch
- ⅛ cup unsweetened cocoa powder
- $1/16$ tsp salt
- 1 large egg whites
- ½ tsp vanilla extract
- ¼ cup chocolate chips

42

Steps:

1. First turn the oven to 350 degrees F to preheat. Line 2 large baking sheets with parchment paper. Coat the paper with cooking spray.
2. Mix powdered sugar, corn-starch cocoa powder, and salt in a medium bowl.
3. Mash the egg whites in a bowl, using a fork or an electric mixer, until a bit firm.
4. Using a rubber spatula, stir in the vanilla and cocoa powder mixture until mixd. Stir in the chocolate chips (or pieces).
5. Use the spoons to drop the dough into the prepared baking sheets, leaving about 2 inches of space between each cookie. Bake one baking sheet at a time until cookies start to crack on top, 12 to 14 minutes.
6. Let cool slightly in the pan before placing it on a wire rack to cool completely.

Per serving:

Calories: 67; Total Fat: 1.8g; Cholesterol: 1mg; Sodium: 28mg; Total Carbohydrate: 12.3g; Dietary Fiber: 0.6g; Total Sugars: 10.1g; Protein: 1.1g

---

41. Chocolate Biscotti with Walnuts

Tot time: 20 Minutes

Preparation time: 5 Minutes

Cooking Time: 15 Minutes

Servings: 12

What you need:

- 1 -¼ cups whole wheat flour
- 1 cup coconut sugar
- 3/2 cup unsweetened cocoa powder
- eggs
- ½ tsp vanilla extract
- ½ tsp baking soda
- ¼ tsp salt
- ½ cup walnuts

Steps:

1. Preheat the oven to 180 ° F.
2. Mix the ingredients except the walnuts in a bowl. Mix well with a spoon.
3. Add walnuts until well mixd.
4. The dough should be a bit thick and sticky.
5. Place the first half of the dough on a 10 x 15-inch baking sheet coated with nonstick spray. Form a slightly rounded 4-by-12- inch rod about ¾ of an inch thick.

6. Repeat the same with the second half of the dough. Put it on a second baking sheet and bake for 30 min.
7. Remove the sheets out of the oven and reduce the temperature to 170 ° F. Let the cookies cool for 20 to 25 min, then cut them into ½-inch-thick slices.
8. Place the cut slices face down on the baking sheet and bake for another 15 min.
9. Flip the cookies to the other side and bake for another 15 min or until very crisp.

Per serving:

Calories: 85; Total Fat: 5.3g; Cholesterol: 27mg; Sodium: 118mg; Total Carbohydrate: 9.9g; Dietary Fiber: 4.3g; Total Sugars 0.4g; Protein: 4.7g

---

42. Chilled Banana Pudding

Tot time: 40 Minutes

Preparation time: 20 Minutes

Cooking Time: 20 Minutes

Servings: 4

What you need:

- ½ cup coconut sugar
- ¼ cup corn-starch
- 1 egg, beaten
- ½ (12 fluid ounce) can heavy cream
- ¾ cups coconut milk
- 1 tsp vanilla extract
- ½ (12 ounces) package vanilla wafers or your choice
- 2 bananas, sliced

Steps:

1. Over a medium heat in a saucepan, mix the coconut sugar, potato starch, egg, heavy cream, and coconut milk. Mix well and stir until thickened. Remove the stove, add the vanilla and mix well.
2. Put a layer of cookies in a large bowl or saucepan. Pour the pudding over the cookies.
3. Garnish it with a layer of banana slices. Place in the refrigerator until it cools.

Per serving:

Calories: 261; Total Fat: 14.2g; Cholesterol: 49mg; Sodium: 60mg; Total Carbohydrate: 31.6g; Dietary Fiber: 2.8g; Total Sugars: 12.7g; Protein: 3.7g

Preparation time: 5 Minutes

Cooking Time: 10 Minutes

Servings: 4

What you need:

- 2 medium zucchinis, cut into ¼-inch slices
- ½ cup seasoned panko bread crumbs
- ⅛ tsp ground black pepper
- 2 tbsp grated Parmesan cheese
- 2 egg whites

Steps:

1. Preheat the oven to 245 ° F.
2. Mix breadcrumbs, pepper, and Parmesan cheese in a small bowl. Put the egg whites in another dish.
3. First, start dipping zucchinis into the egg whites, then coat them with breadcrumbs.
4. Place them on a greased baking sheet.
5. Bake in the oven for approx. 5 minutes, then flip them around and bake another 5 to 10 minutes until golden yellow and crisp.

Per serving:

Calories: 127; Total Fat: 4g; Cholesterol: 10mg; Sodium: 420mg; Total Carbohydrate: 14.2g; Dietary Fiber: 1.8g; Total Sugars: 2.7g; Protein: 9.6g

---

44. Nutmeg- Apricots with Oatmeal Cookies

Preparation time: 5 Minutes

Cooking Time: 15 Minutes

Servings: 12

What you need:

- ½ cup all-purpose flour
- ½ tsp baking powder
- ½ tsp ground nutmeg
- ¼ tsp salt
- ½ cup coconut sugar
- 3 tbsp coconut oil

- 1 large egg
- 1 tsp vanilla extract
- ½ cup old-fashioned rolled oats
- ¼ cup apricots

Steps:

1. Preheat the oven to 350° F.
2. Now coat a baking sheet lightly with cooking spray.
3. Whisk together all-purpose flour, baking powder, nutmeg, and salt in a medium bowl.
4. Whisk together the coconut sugar, coconut oil, egg, and vanilla in a bowl.
5. Add the flour mixture, oats, and apricots and stir with a wooden spoon until mixd.
6. Place flat dough balls on the prepared baking sheet and bake 12 cookies per set.
7. Bake, 12 to 14 minutes until the bottom is golden. Allow the baking sheet to cool for 5 minutes before transferring it to a wire rack to finish cooling. Repeat with the rest of the dough.

Per serving:

Calories: 83; Total Fat: 3.8g; Cholesterol: 23 mg; Sodium: 79mg; Total Carbohydrate: 9.6g; Dietary Fiber: 0.9g; Total Sugars: 0.4g; Protein: 2.3g

---

45. Banana Walnut Pancakes

Tot time: 15 Minutes

Preparation time: 10 Minutes

Cooking Time: 5 Minutes

Servings: 2

What you need:

- 1 large banana
- 2 medium eggs, beaten
- pinch of baking powder
- splash of vanilla extract
- 1 tsp oil
- ¼ cup walnuts, roughly chopped
- ½ cup blueberry

Steps:

1. Grab a bowl. Mash banana with a fork.
2. Add 2 beaten eggs, a pinch of baking powder, and a pinch of vanilla extract.

3. Heat a large non-stick skillet or pancake over medium heat and brush with ½ tsp of oil.
4. With half the batter, pour two pancakes into the pan, cook 1 to 2 minutes per side, then pour onto a plate. Repeat the process with another half tsp of oil and the rest of the dough.
5. Top pancakes with walnuts and blueberries.

Per serving:

Calories: 267; Total Fat: 16.2g; Cholesterol: 164mg; Sodium: 63mg; Total Carbohydrate: 23.1g; Dietary Fiber: 3.7g; Total Sugars: 12.7g; Protein: 10.3g

---

46. Barley Oats Granola with Almond

Tot time: 35 Minutes

Preparation time: 5 Minutes

Cooking Time: 30 Minutes

Servings: 12

What you need:

- 1 cup rolled oats
- ½ cup barley uncooked
- ½ cup almond chopped
- ¼ cup chia seeds
- ⅛ tsp salt
- 3 tbsp coconut oil melted
- 3 tbsp stevia
- 1 tsp pure vanilla extract
- ¼ cup coconut flakes unsweetened

Steps:

1. Turn the oven to 325°F. Line a baking sheet with parchment paper or a silicone mat.
2. Add the oats, barley, almond, chia seeds, and salt to a medium bowl. Stir to mix. Add the oil, stevia, and vanilla extract. Mix well. Spread on the baking sheet.
3. Bake for 25 minutes on a third rack from the bottom, then sprinkle with coconut flakes and cook for another 5 minutes.
4. Take the barley granola out of the oven, let it cool completely (do not touch it), then break it into pieces.

Per serving:

Calories: 137; Total Fat: 6.7g; Cholesterol: 0mg; Sodium: 26mg; Total Carbohydrate: 16.9g; Dietary Fiber: 2.9g; Total Sugars: 4.8g; Protein: 2.9g

Tot time: 35 Minutes

Preparation time: 5 Minutes

Cooking Time: 30 Minutes

Servings: 12

What you need:

- 2 cups cooked quinoa
- 2 large eggs
- ½ cup coconut milk
- ¼ cup applesauce unsweetened
- ¼ cup coconut oil melted
- ¼ cup honey
- ½ cup cacao powder
- 1 tsp pure vanilla extract
- 1 tsp baking powder
- ¼ tsp pink salt
- 1 cup coconut flour
- ½ cup coconut flakes unsweetened
- ¼ cup chocolate chips

Steps:

1. First preheat the oven to 375 degrees F, line the muffin pan with a liner or use a silicone muffin pan.
2. Beat the eggs in a large bowl.
3. Add the coconut milk, applesauce, coconut oil, honey, cocoa powder, vanilla extract, baking powder, and salt; easy to mix. Add chilled quinoa, coconut flour, coconut flakes, and chocolate chips; mix well to mix.
4. Divide the dough into 12 openings with a large ice cream scoop.
5. Bake for 20 minutes, then let sit for 15 minutes to cool down.

Per serving:

Calories: 230; Total Fat: 10.5g; Cholesterol: 32mg; Sodium: 29mg; Total Carbohydrate: 30.1g; Dietary Fiber: 3.9g; Total Sugars: 8.3g; Protein: 6.4g

Tot time: 20 Minutes

Preparation time: 5 Minutes

Cooking Time: 15 Minutes

Servings: 24

What you need:

- ¾ cup honey
- 1 cup quinoa
- ½ cup natural almond butter
- Flax seeds for garnish

Steps:

1. Mix the honey, quinoa, and almond butter in a food processor and process until very finely chopped.
2. Roll into 24 balls (a scant tbsp each).
3. Garnish with flax seeds, if desired.

Per serving:

Calories: 60; Total Fat: 0.6g; Cholesterol: 0mg; Sodium: 1mg; Total Carbohydrate: 13.3g; Dietary Fiber: 0.6g; Total Sugars: 8.7g; Protein: 1.1g

---

49. Almond Barley Pudding

Tot time: 35 Minutes

Preparation time: 10 Minutes

Cooking Time: 25 Minutes

Servings: 8

What you need:

- 2 cups almond milk
- 1 cup barley
- ½ cup raisins
- ½ cup honey
- 2-3 tsp freshly grated lemon zest
- 1 tsp vanilla extract
- Pinch salt
- Ground cinnamon for dusting (optional)

Steps:

1. Mix almond milk, barley, raisins, and honey in a medium heavy saucepan. Bring to a boil while stirring.

2. Lower the heat and simmer, uncovered, while frequently stirring, until the barley is tender and the pudding is creamy (20 to 25 minutes). Stir almost constantly towards the end to avoid burns.
3. Add the lemon zest, vanilla, and salt and pour the pudding into a bowl or individual bowls. Let cool slightly.
4. Eat immediately or eat when cooled.
5. Sprinkle with some cinnamon if desired.

Per serving:

Calories: 383; Total Fat: 22g; Cholesterol: 0mg; Sodium: 38mg; Total Carbohydrate: 46.9g; Dietary Fiber: 6.5g; Total Sugars: 26.1g; Protein: 5.3g

---

50. Pecans-Cinnamon Pumpkin Custards

Tot time: 30 Minutes

Preparation time: 10 Minutes

Cooking Time: 20 Minutes

Servings: 4

What you need:

- ½ cup coconut milk
- ½ cup canned pumpkin
- 1 egg, lightly beaten
- ½ cup honey
- ¼ cup refrigerated or frozen egg product (thawed before use)
- 1 tsp vanilla
- ½ tsp ground cinnamon
- ⅛ tsp salt
- ⅛ tsp ground allspice
- ⅛ cup chopped pecans
- ⅛ cup quinoa
- ½ tbsp butter, melted

Steps:

1. Turn the oven to350 degrees F for preheat. Brush eight 6-ounce ramekins with cooking spray. Place the ramekins in two 2-liter square saucepans.
2. Mix coconut milk, pumpkin, eggs, honey, egg products, and vanilla in a medium bowl. Sift ½ tsp ground cinnamon, salt, and allspice into a small bowl. Add seasoning mix to pumpkin mixture; beat with a whisk until everything is mixd.
3. In the small bowl with the spice mix, mix the nuts, quinoa, brown sugar, and the remaining ¼ tsp ground cinnamon. Add the melted butter; Stir until everything is well mixd.

4. Distribute the pumpkin mixture evenly over prepared dishes. Place the cooking utensils on the rack so that there is enough boiling water in the baking tins up to the middle of the sides of the tins. Bake for 15 minutes.
5. Carefully pour about 1 tbsp of the nut mixture over each. Bake for another 15 to 20 minutes or until a knife comes out clean near the center.
6. Take out shapes from the water; let cool on the rack for 30 minutes. Cover and refrigerate for approx. 4 hours before serving.
7. To serve, top with whipped dessert and, if desired, sprinkle with freshly grated nutmeg.

Per serving:

Calories: 271; Total Fat: 10.4g; Cholesterol: 45mg; Sodium: 139mg; Total Carbohydrate: 43.3g; Dietary Fiber: 2.2g; Total Sugars: 37.1g; Protein: 4.9g

---

51. Mini Fruit Pizzas with Pears

Tot time: 10 Minutes

Preparation time: 10 Minutes

Cooking Time: N/A

Servings: 4

What you need:

- 1 pear, sliced crosswise into 4 slices (¼ inch thick), seeds removed
- 4 tbsp peanut butter
- 4 tbsp mini chocolate chips
- 2 tsp chopped salted roasted almonds
- 2 tsp maple syrup
- A few graham crackers

Steps:

1. Brush each pears slice with 1 tbsp of peanut butter.
2. Lay on top of the cracker.
3. Garnish with 1 tbsp of chocolate chips, ½ tsp of almonds, and ½ tsp of maple syrup.

Per serving:

Calories: 154; Total Fat: 9.7g; Cholesterol: 0mg; Sodium: 95mg; Total Carbohydrate: 14.4g; Dietary Fiber: 2.2g; Total Sugars: 8.7g; Protein: 4.6g

---

52. Blueberry Oats Bars

Tot time: 10 Minutes

Preparation time: 10 Minutes

Cooking Time: N/A

Servings: 8

What you need:

- ½ cup almond flour
- 6 tbsp. coconut oil
- ¼ cup plus 1 tablespoon, coconut sugar, divided
- ⅛ cup toasted walnuts, roughly chopped
- ½ cup old-fashioned rolled oats, divided
- ¼ tsp baking soda
- ¼ tsp kosher salt
- 1 (6-ounce) container of fresh blueberries

Steps:

1. Preheat the oven to 375 ° F.
2. Line an 8-inch pan with baking paper, leaving a 1-inch overhang on two sides.
3. Mix almond flour, coconut oil, and ¼ cup coconut sugar in a food processor 10 to 12 times until it forms a coarse texture. Transfer ⅓ cup to a bowl and add the walnuts and ¼ cup of oatmeal. Squeeze to form small lumps; fresh.
4. In the food processor, add the baking soda, salt, and the remaining cup of oats to the mixture. Pulse until just incorporated, 12 to 15 times. Press into the bottom of the pan. Bake for 14-16 minutes until golden brown.
5. Crush 1 container of blueberries and the remaining tbsp of coconut sugar in a bowl. Spread over the pre-cooked crust. Spread the remaining blueberries from the bowl and the cooled breadcrumb mixture on top.
6. And bake for 40-45 minutes or until golden on top. Let cool in the saucepan for 30 minutes, then transfer the overhang to the wire rack to cool completely.

Per serving:

Calories: 165; Total Fat: 15.1g; Cholesterol: 0mg; Sodium: 114mg; Total Carbohydrate: 7.1g; Dietary Fiber: 1.6g; Total Sugars: 2.4g; Protein: 2.5g

---

53. Green Tea Maple syrup Frozen Yogurt

Tot time: 10 Minutes

Preparation time: 10 Minutes

Cooking Time: N/A

Servings: 4

What you need:

- 1-½ cup Greek yogurt
- 1 cup half-and-half
- ½ cup coconut sugar
- ¼ cup maple syrup
- 1-½ tbsp matcha green tea powder
- 1 tsp. vanilla extract
- ⅛ tsp salt

Steps:

1. Whip the yogurt half and half with coconut sugar, maple syrup, matcha, vanilla, and salt.
2. Leave to rest for 5 minutes.
3. Beat until the coconut sugar has dissolved. Refrigerate for a few hours or until very cold.
4. Pour the mixture into a bowl of an electric refrigerator and process it according to the manufacturer's instructions.
5. Freeze 1 hour before serving.

Per serving:

Calories: 183; Total Fat: 8g; Cholesterol: 25mg; Sodium: 122mg; Total Carbohydrate: 20.3g; Dietary Fiber: 0.3g; Total Sugars: 14g; Protein: 7.2g

---

54. Blueberry Ice Cream

Tot time: 55 Minutes

Preparation time: 10 Minutes

Cooking Time: 45 Minutes

Servings: 4

What you need:

- ½ lb. frozen blueberries
- ½ cup Sour Cream
- ⅛ cup honey
- ¼ tsp. vanilla extract
- Blueberries for garnish

Steps:

1. Finely chop ¼ frozen blueberries with the blade of a knife. Transfer the berries to a metal bowl.

2. In a food processor, chop the remaining ¾ of frozen blueberries, add sour cream, honey, and vanilla and mix until smooth.
3. Transfer in a bowl with the chopped blueberries. Stir until everything is well mixd.
4. Cover and freeze for about 1 hour. It should be firm but not too hard. Garnish with fresh blueberries.

Per serving:

Calories: 127; Total Fat: 6.2g; Cholesterol: 13mg; Sodium: 16mg; Total Carbohydrate: 18.2g; Dietary Fiber: 1.4g; Total Sugars: 14.4g; Protein: 1.4g

---

55. Baked Pears with Quinoa

Tot time: 1 Hour & 5 Minutes

Prep time: 20 Minutes

Cook time: 45 Minutes

Servings: 4

What you need:

- 4 pears, bottoms sliced, so pears stand
- ½ fresh lime halved
- tbsp unsalted butter
- tbsp coconut sugar
- $^1/_{16}$ tsp ground cinnamon
- Pinch ground black pepper
- ½ cup rice wine
- ½ cup coconut milk, heated
- 1 tsp finely grated lime zest
- 1 cup cooked quinoa
- Low-fat plain yogurt

Steps:

1. Turn the oven to 375 ° F for preheat. Slice the top third of each pear. Hollow out the pear meat using a spoon, 2 inches in diameter.
2. Rub the cut part with lime and place the pears in a 9-inch square baking dish. Cut the carved parts of the pears without seeds and save them.
3. Melt the coconut oil in a small saucepan, add 2 tbsp of coconut sugar, cinnamon, and pepper, and cook until smooth.
4. Brush the inside of the pears with the oil mixture. Pour the rice wine into the bottom of the baking dish. Cover the plate with foil and bake for about 30 min, until the pears are tender.

5. Remove the foil and cook for a further 5 min. Transfer the pears to a dish. Carefully filter the cooking liquid into a small saucepan and bring it to a boil.
6. Cook 5 min until everything is reduced and thickened.
7. While the pears cook, mix the hot milk, the remaining coconut sugar, the reserved chopped pears, and the lime zest in the hot quinoa and cook for a few minutes.
8. Spread the quinoa over the baked pears.
9. Top each pear with a tbsp of yogurt and drizzle with reduced rice wine.

Per serving:

Calories: 521; Total Fat: 15.8g; Cholesterol: 15mg; Sodium: 340mg; Total Carbohydrate: 90g; Dietary Fiber: 10.4g; Total Sugars: 29.5g; Protein: 8.3g

---

56. Red Dragon Fruit Sorbet

Tot time: 15 Minutes

Preparation time: 10 Minutes

Cooking Time: 5 Minutes

Servings: 4

What you need:

- ½ cup maple syrup
- ¼ cup water
- ⅛ cup lime juice
- 1-½ cups cubed red dragon fruit

Steps:

1. Mix maple syrup, water, and lime juice in a saucepan over medium heat; cook, about 5 minutes.
2. Remove from the heat and refrigerate for about 30 minutes.
3. Puree the red dragon fruit in a mixer or food processor.
4. Add the mashed red dragon fruit to the syrup mixture. Transfer the red dragon fruit mixture to an ice cream maker and freeze according to the manufacturer's instructions.

Per serving:

Calories: 116; Total Fat: 0.1g; Cholesterol: 0mg; Sodium: 5mg; Total Carbohydrate: 30g; Dietary Fiber: 0.3g; Total Sugars: 26.5g; Protein: 0.1g

---

57. Papaya and Mint Sorbet

Tot time: 10 Minutes

Preparation time: 10 Minutes

Cooking Time: N/A

Servings: 8

What you need:

- 1 papaya - peeled, cored, and cut into chunks
- ¼ cup coconut sugar
- ¼ cup pineapple juice
- ⅛ cup mint leaves

Steps:

1. Mix the papaya, coconut sugar, pineapple juice, and mint in a mixer until smooth.
2. Chill for 1 hour in the refrigerator.
3. Place the mixture in an ice maker and mix it according to the manufacturer's instructions.
4. Store in an airtight container and freeze for 8 hours or overnight.

Per serving:

Calories: 25; Cholesterol: 0mg; Total Fat: 0.1g; Sodium: 5mg; Total Carbohydrate: 6g; Dietary Fiber: 0.8g; Total Sugars: 3.9g; Protein: 0.3g

---

58. Gingerbread Balls

Tot time: 10 Minutes

Preparation time: 10 Minutes

Cooking Time: N/A

Servings: 10

What you need:

- ½ cup gluten-free rolled oats
- ¼ cup all-purpose flour
- ½ tbsp ground cinnamon
- ½ tsp ground ginger
- ¼ tsp ground nutmeg
- ¼ tsp vanilla extract
- 1 cup figs, pitted and chopped
- 1-½ tbsp powdered white sugar

Steps:

1. Put the oatmeal, all-purpose flour, cinnamon, ginger, nutmeg, and vanilla extract in a mixer.
2. Stir well until smooth. Mix the dates in batches until smooth paste forms.
3. Form 1-inch balls and roll in the powdered white sugar.

Per serving:

Calories: 40; Total Fat: 0.4g; Cholesterol: 0mg; Sodium: 0mg; Total Carbohydrate: 8.4g; Dietary Fiber: 1g; Total Sugars: 2.3g; Protein: 1.1g

---

59. Paleo Sweet Potato Snack Bowl

Tot time: 65 Minutes

Preparation time: 5 Minutes

Cooking Time: 60 Minutes

Makes: 1

What you need:

- 1 medium sweet potato, scrubbed, poked with a fork
- ½ teaspoon cinnamon
- 2 tablespoons chopped toasted walnuts
- 2 tablespoons toasted pumpkin seeds

Steps:

1. Preheat your oven to 350 degrees. Arrange the sweet potato on a paper-lined baking sheet and bake for 60 minutes or until tender; let cool and then mash together with cinnamon.
2. Transfer the mashed potatoes to a serving bowl and serve topped with chopped toasted walnuts and pumpkin seeds.

Per serving:

Calories: 297; Total Fat: 11.85 g; Net Carbs: 44 g; Dietary Fiber: 8.67 g; Sugars: 8 g; Protein: 6.7 g; Cholesterol: 0 mg; Sodium: 102 mg

---

60. Prunes & Kamut Energy Bars

Tot time: 45 Minutes

Preparation time: 20 Minutes

Cooking Time: 25 Minutes

Makes: 20 Bars

What you need:

- 2/3 cup prunes
- 1½ cups water
- ¾ cup coconut
- ¾ cup Kamut flour
- 1 cup gluten-free large flake oats
- ½ cup dried cranberries
- ½ cup gluten-free dark chocolate cut into slivers (or chocolate chips)
- ½ cup pumpkin seeds, toasted
- ¼ cup hemp hearts
- 1 banana, mashed
- 3 tbsp. maple syrup

Steps:

1. Preheat oven to 350°F. Coat a cookie pan with cooking spray and set it aside.
2. Mix prunes and water in a pot set over medium-high heat; bring to a rolling boil; take from heat and let cool for about 10 minutes.
3. Add coconut in a pan set over medium heat; stir for about 3 minutes or until golden brown. Set aside.
4. In a large bowl, mix pumpkin seeds, chocolate, cranberries, oats, flour, and hemp hearts; stir until well mixd. Stir in maple syrup and mashed banana.
5. Transfer the cooked prunes and cooking water to a food processor and puree until very smooth; add the prune puree to the other ingredients and stir to mix. Move the mixture to the pan and bake for about 30 minutes. Remove from oven and let cool before cutting into 20 equal squares. Have a healthy meal!

Per serving:

Calories: 287; Total Fat: 10.8 g; Carbs: 43.3 g; Dietary Fiber: 5.6 g; Sugars: 18 g; Protein: 6.9 g; Cholesterol: 2 mg; Sodium: 14 mg

---

61. Spiced Apple Crisps

Tot time: 35 Minutes

Preparation time: 1 Minute

Cooking Time: 25 Minutes

Makes: 4

What you need:

- 4 apples, sliced
- 3 tablespoons raw honey
- ½ teaspoon sea salt

- 2 teaspoon cinnamon
- 1 cup virgin olive oil
- 1 teaspoon black pepper

Steps:

1. In a large bowl, stir together cinnamon, raw honey, black pepper, and sea salt until well mixed; add the apple slices into the mixture and toss to coat well.
2. Heat olive oil in a skillet over medium heat; add in the apple slices and deep fry until golden browned. Drain the apple crisps onto paper towel-lined plates and serve with a cup of tea.

Per serving:

Calories: 413 Total Fat: 21.3 g; Carbs: 33.8 g; Dietary Fiber: 6.8 g; Sugars: 22.3 g; Protein: 3.9 g; Cholesterol: 0 mg; Sodium: 321 mg

---

62. Beef & Millet Stuffed Peppers

Tot time: Hour 20 Minutes

Preparation time: 20 Minutes

Cooking Time: 1 Hour

Makes: 4

What you need:

- 4 red bell peppers, tops removed
- ½ cup millet
- ½ pound ground beef
- 2 tablespoons olive oil
- 2 cups water
- 1 onion, chopped
- 2 garlic cloves, crushed
- 3 tablespoons tomato paste
- 1 tablespoon chopped cilantro
- ¼ teaspoon cayenne pepper
- 1 teaspoon cumin
- 1 teaspoon paprika
- ¼ teaspoon black pepper

Steps:

1. Turn the oven to 450°F for preheat and coat a baking dish.
2. In a saucepan, mix millet and water and bring to a gentle boil; turn the heat to low and cook for about 15 minutes, or until the water is absorbed.

3. Heat the olive oil in a pan over medium heat and sauté the red onion and garlic for approximately 5 minutes, or until soft. stir in ground beef and cook for about 10 minutes or until browned. Stir in cayenne, cumin, tomato paste, paprika, and black pepper and cook for 5 minutes.
4. Stir in the cooked millet and cilantro until well mixd; spoon into the bell peppers and arrange them in the greased baking dish; bake in the preheated oven for about 20 minutes or until the pepper are tender.

Per serving:

Calories: 325; Total Fat: 1.4 g; Net Carbs: 28 g; Dietary Fiber: 5.2 g; Sugars: 8.7 g; Protein: 22.3 g; Cholesterol: 51 mg; Sodium: 60 mg

63. Avocado & Pea Dip with Carrots

Tot time: 10 Minutes

Preparation time: 10 Minutes

Cooking Time: N/A

Makes: 6

What you need:

- 1 avocado, peeled and seed removed
- 1 1/2 cups steamed snow peas
- 1/4 teaspoon cayenne pepper
- 2 tablespoons lime juice
- I clove of garlic, diced
- Carrots to serve

Steps:

1. Mix together all ingredients in a mixer and mix until very smooth. Serve with fresh carrots.

Per serving:

Calories: 80; Total Fat: 3.9 g; Carbs: 9.3 g; Dietary Fiber: 4.1 g; Sugars: 2.9 g; Protein: 3.1 g; Cholesterol: 0 mg; Sodium: 4 mg

64. Chili-lime Cucumber, Jicama, &Pineapple Sticks

Tot time: 5 Minutes

Preparation time: 5 Minutes

Cooking Time: N/A

Makes: 2

What you need:

- 6 spears of cucumber
- 6 spears of very ripe pineapple
- 6 spears jicama (you can use mango instead)
- 1 teaspoon chili lime seasoning
- 2 lime wedges

Steps:

1. In a bowl, mix together cucumber, pineapple, jicama, lime juice, chili lime seasoning until well mixd.
2. Serve garnished with lime wedges. Have a healthy meal!

Per serving:

Calories: 17; Total Fat: 0 g; Carbs: 4.3 g; Dietary Fiber: 1 g; Sugars: 2 g; Protein: 0 g; Cholesterol: 0 mg; Sodium: 11 mg

---

65. Raw Turmeric Cashew Nut & Coconut Balls

Tot time: 10 Minutes

Preparation time: 10 Minutes

Cooking Time: N/A

Makes: 12

What you need:

- 1 cup raw cashews
- 1 1/2 cup shredded coconut
- 1tablespoon raw honey
- 3 teaspoons ground turmeric
- 1 teaspoon cinnamon
- 1 teaspoon ground ginger
- 1 teaspoon black pepper
- 1/2 teaspoon sea salt

Steps:

1. In a food processor, process coconut until almost oily; add the rest of the ingredients and process until cashews are finely chopped.
2. Press the mixture into bite-sized balls and arrange them on a baking tray.
3. Refrigerate until firm before serving.

Per serving:

Calories: 131; Total Fat: 10 g; Carbs: 7.3 g; Dietary Fiber: 4.9 g; Sugars: 2.7 g; Protein: 2.5 g; Cholesterol: 0 mg; Sodium: 92 mg

---

66. Spiced and Creamed Corn Snack

Tot time: 20 Minutes

Preparation time: 10 Minutes

Cooking Time: 10 Minutes

Makes: 4

What you need:

- 2 cup corn kernels
- 2 tablespoons chopped red bell pepper
- 1 tablespoon chopped green chili
- 2 tablespoons chopped cilantro
- ½ teaspoon cumin seeds
- 1 teaspoon oil
- 2 tablespoons coconut cream
- 1 teaspoon lemon juice
- ½ teaspoon salt

Steps:

1. Lightly grease a heavy pan with oil and then fry in corn kernels for about 5 minutes or until lightly browned; take from heat and stir in cumin seed powder, salt, red bell pepper, green chili cilantro, coconut cream, and lemon juice.
2. Mix to mix well and serve warm. Have a healthy meal!

Per serving:

Calories: 173; Total Fat: 9.3 g; Carbs: 16.2 g; Dietary Fiber: 3 g; Sugars: 6.1 g; Protein: 5.6 g; Cholesterol: 24 mg; Sodium: 467 mg

---

67. Carrot and Parsnips French Fries

Tot time: 35 Minutes

Preparation time: 15 Minutes

Cooking Time: 20 Minutes

Makes: 2

What you need:

- 6 large carrots
- 6 large parsnips
- 2 tablespoons extra virgin olive oil
- ½ teaspoon sea salt

Steps:

1. Chop the carrots and parsnips into 2-inch sections and then cut each section into thin sticks.
2. Toss together the carrots and parsnip sticks with extra virgin olive oil and salt in a bowl and spread into a baking sheet lined with parchment paper.
3. Bake the sticks at 425° for about 20 minutes or until browned.

Per serving:

Calories: 209; Total Fat: 14 g; Carbs: 21.2 g; Dietary Fiber: 5.3 g; Protein: 1.8 g; Cholesterol: 0 mg; Sodium: 617 mg; Sugars: 10.6 g

---

68. Dry-Roasted Chickpea

Tot time: 54 Minutes

Preparation time: 10 Minutes

Cooking Time: 44 Minutes

Makes: 8

What you need:

- 2 cups chickpeas
- 2 teaspoons extra-virgin olive oil
- 1/4 teaspoon salt
- ¼ teaspoon black pepper

Steps:

1. Preheat oven to 425°F. Spread chickpeas in a medium baking dish and pat them dry with a paper towel; bake, stirring halfway through, for about 22 minutes.
2. Move to a large bowl and toss with olive oil, sea salt, and pepper; return to oven and bake, stirring halfway through, for another 22 minutes or until dry and golden.

Per serving:

Calories: 256; Total Fat: 5.6 g; Carbs: 20.2 g; Dietary Fiber: 11.6 g; Sugars: 7.1 g; Protein: 12.9 g; Cholesterol: 0 mg; Sodium: 113 mg

Tot time: 1 Hour 10 Minutes

Preparation time: 10 Minutes

Cooking Time: 1 Hour

Makes: 5

What you need:

- 1/4 cup amaranth
- 1/4 cup flaxseeds
- 1 tablespoon sesame seeds
- 2 tablespoons black chia seeds
- 1/2 cup sunflower seeds
- 1/4 cup pepitas
- 3/4 cup warm water
- 1 teaspoon sea salt

Steps:

1. In a bowl, mix together amaranth, seeds, and pepitas; add warm water and sit until all water is absorbed. Stir in salt and pepper.
2. Meanwhile, preheat your oven to 320 degrees and line a baking tray with paper.
3. Spread the amaranth mixture onto the tray and bake in the oven for about 1 hour or until golden and crispy. Cut into 20 bars and serve.

Nutrition per **Makes:**

Calories: 255; Total Fat: 4.4 g; Carbs: 2.6 g; Dietary Fiber: 2 g; Sugars: 0.2 g; Protein: 2.5 g; Cholesterol: 0 mg; Sodium: 107 mg

---

70. Superfood Trail Mix

Tot time: 5 Minutes

Preparation time: 5 Minutes

Cooking Time: N/A

Makes: 5

What you need:

- ¼ cup unsalted roasted peanuts
- ¼ cup whole shelled almonds
- ¼ cup chopped pitted dates

- ¼ cup dried cranberries
- 2 ounces dried apricots

Steps:

1. In a medium bowl, mix all the ingredients until well mixd. Have a healthy meal!

Nutrition per **Makes:**

Calories: 132; Total Fat: 7 g; Carbs: 15 g; Dietary Fiber: 3 g; Sodium: 0 mg Sugars: 10 g; Protein: 4 g; Cholesterol: 0 mg;

---

71. Ginger Tahini Dip with Assorted Veggies

Tot time: 5 Minutes

Preparation time: 5 Minutes

Cooking Time: N/A

Makes: 8

What you need:

- ½ cup tahini
- 1 teaspoon grated garlic
- 2 teaspoons ground turmeric
- 1 tablespoon grated fresh ginger
- ¼ cup apple cider vinegar
- ¼ cup water
- ½ teaspoon salt

Steps:

1. Whisk together tahini, turmeric, ginger, water, vinegar, garlic, and salt in a bowl until well mixed. Serve with assorted veggies.

Per serving:

Calories: 92; Total Fat: 8 g; Carbs: 4 g; Cholesterol: 0 mg; Dietary Fiber: 1 g; Sugars: 0 g; Protein: 3 g; Sodium: 151 mg;

---

72. Spiced Mango Trial Mix

Tot time: 5 Minutes

Preparation time: 5 Minutes

Cooking Time: N/A

Makes: 1

What you need:

- 2 tablespoons chopped toasted cashews
- 2 tablespoons chopped toasted Brazil nuts
- 2 tablespoons toasted peanuts
- ¼ cup dried mango
- 2 tablespoons toasted coconut flakes
- 1 teaspoon cinnamon
- 1 teaspoon cumin
- 1 teaspoon chili powder

Steps:

1. Mix everything and Have a healthy meal!

Per serving:

Calories: 457; Total Fat: 32 g; Carbs: 34 g; Dietary Fiber: 19 g; Sugars: 13 g; Protein: 14 g; Cholesterol: 0 mg; Sodium: 221 mg

Main Courses

---

73. Ginger Tempeh and Vegetable Stir-Fry

Preparation time: 10 Minutes

Cooking Time: 30 Minutes

Servings: 6

What you need:

- 1 block Tempeh
- ¾ cup Coconut aminos
- ½ cup lime juice
- 2 tbsp fresh ginger minced
- 4 tbsp coconut oil (or olive oil)
- 1 cup zucchini, chopped
- 1 cup cauliflower, chopped
- 2 parsnips, sliced
- 1 onion, chopped
- red bell pepper, sliced
- 1 cup asparagus, sliced
- 1 cup eggplant, sliced,
- 1 leek, sliced
- 1 cup cooked quinoa

Steps:

1. Cut the tempeh into 1-inch cubes.
2. In a large shallow bowl, mix the coconut aminos, lime juice, and ginger. Marinate the tempeh in this sauce for at least 1 hour. If need to cook the quinoa, do so at this point.
3. In a wok or large skillet, add the coconut oil and cook the zucchini, cauliflower, parsnips, onions, red peppers, and tempeh over high heat, stirring frequently.
4. Add the asparagus, eggplant, leek, and tempeh marinade. Simmer a few more minutes. But the vegetables should be tender but not mushy. Add the quinoa and cook until heated through and well mixd. Serve and enjoy.

Per serving:

Calories: 441; Total Fat: 1.5g; Cholesterol: 0mg; Sodium: 146mg; Total Carbohydrate: 57.5g; Dietary Fiber: 8.7g; Total Sugars: 8.7g; Protein: 14.5g

Preparation time: 15 Minutes

Cooking Time: 20 Minutes

Servings: 4

What you need:

- 2 tbsp Coconut aminos
- 1 tbsp apple cider vinegar
- 1 tbsp minced fresh ginger root
- 1 large clove garlic, minced
- 4 (6 ounces) turkey breast
- 1 tbsp olive oil

Steps:

1. Mix coconut aminos, apple cider vinegar, ginger, and garlic in a shallow bowl. Put the turkey breast in the marinade and turn it over to coat it. Cover the plate and refrigerate for at least 30 to 45 minutes.
2. Preheat the grill.
3. Remove the breast out of the marinade.
4. Discard any remaining liquid. Coat both sides of the meat with oil.
5. Cook the turkey breast on the preheated grill, 10 to 15 minutes per side, until cooked through.
6. Serve with herbs, rice, or veggies of your choice.

Per serving:

Calories: 217; Total Fat: 6.3g; Cholesterol: 73mg; 24% Sodium: 1735mg; Total Carbohydrate: 9.1g; Dietary Fiber: 0.9g; Total Sugars: 6g; Protein: 29.1g

75. Sautéed Turkey and Cabbage

Preparation time: 20 Minutes

Cooking Time: 20 Minutes

Servings: 4

What you need:

- 2 turkey breasts, skinless, boneless, and sliced
- 1 head of cabbage, shredded
- 2 carrots, shredded
- 3 tbsp paprika

- 3 tomatoes, pureed
- 1 cup chicken stock
- 2 tbsp coconut oil
- sea salt and freshly ground black pepper

Steps:

1. Heat the coconut oil in a skillet over medium heat.
2. Cook the turkey slices until golden brown on each side.
3. When you are almost done, add the shredded cabbage and carrots to the pan and cook, stirring, for 4-5 minutes.
4. Add the tomatoes, chicken broth, paprika, and season to taste.
5. Stir the content well, then bring it to a boil.
6. Turn the heat to low and simmer for 10-12 minutes to ensure the turkey is cooked through.
7. Remove from the heat and serve hot.

Per serving:

Calories: 172; Total Fat: 8.3g; Cholesterol: 9mg; Sodium: 469mg; Total Carbohydrate: 20.9g; Dietary Fiber: 8.4g; Total Sugars: 11.1g; Protein: 7.9g

---

76. Ginger Glazed Tuna

Preparation time: 5 Minutes

Cooking Time: 15 Minutes

Servings: 2

What you need:

- 1-½ tbsp maple syrup
- 1-½ tbsp coconut aminos
- 1-½ tbsp apple cider vinegar
- ½ tsp grated fresh ginger root
- ½ tsp garlic powder
- 1 tsp coconut oil
- 2 (6 ounces) tuna fillets
- salt and pepper to taste
- ½ tbsp avocado oil

Steps:

1. Mix the maple syrup, coconut aminos, apple cider vinegar, ginger, garlic powder, and coconut oil in a small glass bowl.
2. Place the fillets on a plate and sprinkle salt and pepper. Cover to marinate and refrigerate for 20 minutes.

3. Heath the oil in a skillet over medium heat. Remove the fish from the plate and keep the marinade. Bake the fish on a pan for 4 to 6 minutes per side, turning it just once, until tender.
4. Place the steaks on a platter. Keep them warm.
5. Heat the remaining marinade into the skillet over medium heat until the mixture is evenly reduced to a glaze.
6. Pour it over the fillets and serve immediately. If desired, serve with some brown rice.

Per serving:

Calories: 88; Total Fat: 2.8g; Cholesterol: 9mg; Sodium: 16mg; Total Carbohydrate: 7.6g; Dietary Fiber: 0.2g; Total Sugars: 6.2g; Protein: 7.7g

---

77. Crispy Lemon- Chili Roasted Kale

Tot time: 30 Minutes

Preparation time: 10 Minutes

Cooking Time: 20 Minutes

Makes: 2

What you need:

- 2 bunches of kale, ribs, and stems removed, roughly chopped
- 2 tablespoons lemon juice
- 2 tablespoons extra-virgin olive oil
- 1 teaspoon lemon salt
- 2 teaspoons chili powder
- Parmesan wedge

Steps:

1. Preheat oven to 250°F. In a large bowl, massage together kale, lemon juice, extra virgin olive oil, lemon salt, and chili powder until kale is tender; spread the kale on a baking sheet and bake for about 20 minutes or until crisp-tender.
2. Take from oven and sprinkle with parmesan cheese. Serve warm.

Per serving:

Calories: 165; Total Fat: 14.6 g; Carbs: 8.7 g; Dietary Fiber: 2 g; Sugars: 0.5 g; Protein: 2.4 g; Cholesterol: 0 mg; Sodium: 58 mg

---

78. Low-Carb Cassava Crepes

Tot time: 25 Minutes

Preparation time: 10 Minutes

Cooking Time: 15 Minutes

Makes: 4

What you need:

- 1 ⅓ cups cassava flour
- 2 egg whites
- 1 cup milk
- 2 teaspoons lemon juice
- 2 tablespoons melted butter
- 1 teaspoon stevia
- 1 pinch salt

Steps:

1. In a mixing bowl, whisk egg whites, milk, lemon juice, butter, stevia, and sea salt; gradually whisk in cassava flour until well mixed and very smooth.
2. Preheat a nonstick pan and spread in about a quarter cup of batter to cover the bottom. Cook for 3 minutes per side or until golden brown.
3. Repeat with the remaining batter. Serve with a cup of tea or a glass of juice.

Per serving:

Calories: 227; Total Fat: 7.5 g; Net Carbs: 38.69 g; Dietary Fiber: 0 g; Sugars: 3.12 g; Protein: 3.65 g; Cholesterol: 22 mg; Sodium: 84 mg

---

79. Healthy Taro Chips

Tot time: 30 Minutes

Preparation time: 10 Minutes

Cooking Time: 20 Minutes

Makes: 4

What you need:

- 1 pound taro peeled
- 1 teaspoon olive oil
- A pinch of salt
- A pinch of pepper

Steps:

1. Slice the taro lengthwise; place the taro slices on paper-lined baking sheets and brush with olive oil.

2. Season with sea salt and pepper and bake at 400 degrees for about 20 minutes or until crisp.

Per serving:

Calories: 137 Total Fat: 1.4 g; Net Carbs: 25.3 g; Dietary Fiber: 4.7 g; Sugars: 0.5 g; Protein: 1.7 g; Cholesterol: 0 mg; Sodium: 51 mg

---

80. Amaranth Pop Corns

Tot time: 15 Minutes

Preparation time: 5 Minutes

Cooking Time: 10 Minutes

Makes: 2

What you need:

- 1/2 cup amaranth seeds
- 1 teaspoon olive oil
- 1 teaspoon cinnamon
- ½ teaspoon sea salt

Steps:

1. Heat olive oil in a pot set over high heat; add the amaranth seeds and cook until they start popping. Cover the pot and let all seeds pop.
2. Serve sprinkled with cinnamon and sea salt.

Per serving:

Calories: 205 Total Fat: 5.5 g; Net Carbs: 28.1 g; Dietary Fiber: 5.1 g; Sugars: 0.8 g; Protein: 7.1 g; Cholesterol: 0 mg; Sodium: 478 mg

---

81. Refreshing Watermelon Mix Popsicles

Tot time: 10 Minutes

Preparation time: 10 Minutes

Cooking Time: 0 Minutes

Makes: 6

What you need:

- ½ a watermelon, seeds removed
- 1/3 cup honey

- 2 ½ cups water

Steps:

1. Mix all the ingredients and strain to remove the fiber and the form. Transfer to a Popsicle mound and freeze for at least 3 hours.
2. Have a healthy meal!

Per serving:

Calories: 73; Total Fat: 0 g; Net Carbs: 14.3 g; Dietary Fiber: 0.8g; Sugars: 12.1; Protein: 0.5 g; Cholesterol: 0 mg; Sodium: 1.6 mg

---

82. Fizzy Lemon and Strawberry Punch

Yield: 12 Servings

Tot time: 20 Minutes

Preparation time: 20 Minutes

Cooking Time: 0 Minutes

What you need:

- 1 cup honey
- 10 strawberries
- 2 cups freshly squeezed lemon juice
- 7 cups of water

Steps:

1. Mix all the ingredients together; you can divide the ingredients into two or three if your mixer is not big enough.
2. Chill in the fridge and serve cold. Have a healthy meal!

Per serving:

Calories: 141; Total Fat: 0.3 g; Net Carbs: 30.5 g; Dietary Fiber: 2.2; Sugars: 10.9; Protein: 1.1 g; Cholesterol: 0 mg; Sodium: 4 mg

---

83. Yummy Chocolate and Peanut Butter Treats

Tot time: 25Minutes

Preparation time: 25 Minutes

Cooking Time: 0 Minutes

Makes: 8

What you need:

- 1 cup natural peanut butter, melted
- 1 ½ cups almond milk
- 16 whole-grain crackers
- ½ cup dark chocolate chips, melted

Steps:

1. Mix the peanut butter and melted chocolate with the milk and chill in the fridge for 5 minutes.
2. Make a peanut butter chocolate sandwich by spreading the chilled mixture on one side of the crackers and top with another cracker.
3. Cover with cling wrap and put in the freezer for an hour. Have a healthy meal!

Per serving:

Calories: 422; Total Fat: 14 g; Net Carbs: 32 g; Dietary Fiber: 0.1g; Sugars: 5.6; Protein: 8.2 g; Cholesterol: 0 mg; Sodium: 284 mg

---

84. Savory Hummus with Olives

Tot time: 5 Minutes

Preparation time: 5 Minutes

Cooking Time: 0 Minutes

Makes: 8

What you need:

- 1 can black beans, drained, with the liquid reserved
- 1 1.2 tablespoons tahini
- 10 Greek olives
- ½ teaspoon sea salt
- 1 clove garlic, minced
- 2 tablespoon freshly squeezed lemon
- ¼ teaspoon cayenne pepper
- ¼ teaspoon sweet paprika
- ¾ teaspoon cumin powder

Steps:

1. Mix all the ingredients apart from the olives and paprika to a food processor and pulse until well mixd and smooth.
2. Top with olives and paprika. Serve with veggie sticks. Have a healthy meal!

Per serving:

Calories: 81.2; Total Fat: 3.1 g; Net Carbs: 10.5 g; Dietary Fiber: 6.1g; Sugars: 0.7; Protein: 6.1 g; Cholesterol: 0 mg; Sodium: 427 mg

---

85. Healthy Superfood Raw Bars

Tot time: 10 Minutes

Preparation time: 15 Minutes

Cooking Time: 5 Minutes

Makes: 6

What you need:

- 1 /2 cup toasted pistachios
- 1/4 cup goji berries + 2 tablespoons more
- 1 /2 cup roasted almonds
- 1/4 cup chia seeds
- 3 /4 cup blackcurrants
- 3 /4 cup coconut flakes, toasted
- 1 / 3 cup ginger
- 1 tablespoon raw cacao nibs
- 1 tablespoon coconut oil
- 1.1 pound chopped dark chocolate
- Pinch of sea salt

Steps:

1. Prepare a baking pan by greasing and lining it with baking paper. In a large bowl, mix 1/3 cup of pistachios, blackcurrants, ½ cup of coconut flakes, goji berries, almond, chia pieces, and ginger until well mixed.
2. Stir together cacao nibs, the remaining pistachios and coconut flakes, and more goji berries in another bowl. In a saucepan, stir together oil, chocolate, and salt until chocolate is melted.
3. Pour the chocolate mixture into the pistachio mixture and stir until well coated; transfer to the pan and sprinkle with the cacao mixture. Refrigerate for at least 4 hours or until firm. Cut into 24 squares and serve, storing the rest in the refrigerator for two weeks.

Per serving:

Calories: 218; Total Fat: 15 g; Carbs: 18 g; Dietary Fiber: 2 g; Sugars: 13 g; Protein: 3 g; Cholesterol: 0 mg; Sodium: 110 mg

Preparation time: 10 Minutes

Cooking Time: 25 Minutes

Servings: 2

What you need:

- 1 tsp garlic powder
- 2 skinless, turkey breast halves
- salt and ground black pepper to taste
- ½ cup chicken broth
- ½ tbsp lemon juice
- 1 tbsp chopped cilantro

Steps:

1. Place the nonstick skillet over low heat.
2. Season the breast with garlic powder, salt, and pepper and place it on a skillet. Cook over medium heat, 10 to 12 minutes, until golden brown on both sides.
3. Add in the chicken broth. Bring to a boil, then lower to a medium-low heat, add the lemon juice, cover, and cook for 10 to 15 minutes, or until the breast is no longer pink in the center.
4. Place the breast on the serving platter and keep the liquid in the pan. Simmer the liquid for about 3 minutes until slightly reduced. Pour liquid over the breast.
5. Garnish with fresh Cilantro.

Per serving:

Calories: 158; Total Fat: 4.7g; Cholesterol: 65mg; Sodium: 232mg; Total Carbohydrate: 1.4g; Dietary Fiber: 0.2g; Total Sugars: 0.6g; Protein: 26.5g

87. Garlicky Barley and Pinto Beans

Preparation time: 15 Minutes

Cooking Time: 35 Minutes

Servings: 6

What you need:

- ½ tsp coconut oil
- ½ onion, chopped
- 1 tsp garlic powder
- ½ cup barley

- ½ cup vegetable broth
- ½ cup water
- ½ tsp ground cumin
- ¼ tsp cayenne pepper
- salt and ground black pepper to taste
- ½ cup green peas
- ½ cup broccoli
- 1(15 ounces) can of pinto beans, drained and rinsed
- ¼ cup chopped fresh cilantro

Steps:

1. Heat oil in a saucepan over medium heat; cook and stir onion and garlic powder until lightly browned for about 10 minutes.
2. Toss the barley with the onion mixture and top with the vegetable broth and water. Season with cumin, cayenne pepper, salt, and pepper.
3. Bring the mixture to a boil. Cover, reduce the heat, and simmer, about 20 minutes until the barley is tender and the liquid is absorbed.
4. Add the green peas, broccoli, carrot to the pot and simmer for about 5 minutes until heated through. Stir in the pinto beans and cilantro and serve.

Per serving:

Calories: 189; Total Fat: 1.3g; Cholesterol: 0mg; Sodium: 55mg; Total Carbohydrate: 35.2g; Dietary Fiber: 8.9g; Total Sugars: 2.3g; Protein: 9.9g

---

88. Chicken Chili

Preparation time: 15 Minutes

Cooking Time: 30 Minutes

Servings: 8

What you need:

- 2 tbsp vegetable oil
- 2 large onions, chopped
- 1 red bell pepper, seeded and chopped
- 1 green bell pepper, seeded and chopped
- 1 stick of leek, chopped
- 1 carrot, chopped
- 4 garlic cloves (minced)
- 1.5-pound lean ground chicken
- 4 tbsp paprika
- 4 tsp ground cumin
- 1 tsp oregano

- 1tsp ground coriander
- 2 (14.5-ounce) can crushed tomatoes
- 2(8-ounce) can unsalted tomato sauce
- 2 15-ounce cans of pinto beans (drained)
- 8 tbsp fresh cream

Steps:

1. Heat the vegetable oil in a saucepan. Add the onion, leek, red bell pepper, green bell pepper, carrot, and garlic. Cook for 5 mints until onions are translucent.
2. Disintegrate the grounded chicken in the pan and break it up with a wooden spoon. Cook until no longer pink inside, or about 5 minutes.
3. Add the paprika, ground cumin, ground coriander, and oregano.
4. Add the tomato sauce and tomatoes and simmer for 10 min. Stir from time to time.
5. Add the pinto beans, mix well and simmer for another 5 to 10 min.
6. Serve in bowls. Add a tbsp fat-free fresh cream plus a little chopped fresh cilantro if you have it. Serve and Have a healthy meal!

Per serving:

Calories: 602; Total Fat: 10.5g; Cholesterol: 47mg; Sodium: 632mg; Total Carbohydrate: 88.5g; Dietary Fiber: 23.6g; Total Sugars: 14.8g; Protein: 41.9g

---

89. Kale and Cottage Pasta

Preparation time: 5 Minutes

Cooking Time: 15 Minutes

Servings: 4

What you need:

- 1-ounce Gluten Free elbow macaroni or any type
- 1 tsp coconut oil
- ¼ cup onion, finely chopped
- 1 garlic clove, minced
- 5 cups fresh kale, roughly chopped
- ½ ounce fresh parsley, chopped
- ½ cup low-fat cottage cheese
- ⅛ cup coconut milk

Steps:

1. Cook pasta according to package instructions.

2. Now melt the coconut oil in a saucepan over medium heat. Add onion and garlic and sauté until onions are tender and fragrant (about 5 min). Be careful not to brown the garlic.
3. Add parsley and the kale to the pan and stir until tender.
4. Then add the cottage cheese and the coconut milk to the saucepan and stir well.
5. Drain the pasta and keep about ¼ cup of the cooking water.
6. Mix cooked pasta and cottage mixture in a large bowl. If it is too thick, add the cooking water to the mixture.
7. Serve immediately with freshly ground black pepper.

Per serving:

Calories: 125; Total Fat: 3.7g; Cholesterol: 2mg; Sodium: 153mg; Total Carbohydrate: 16.4g; Dietary Fiber: 2.3g; Total Sugars: 0.8g; Protein: 7.7g

90. Chicken Fajita Bowl

Preparation time: 10 Minutes

Cooking Time: 10 Minutes

Servings: 4

What you need:

- 1 ½ tsp oregano
- 1 tbsp chili powder
- ½ tsp garlic, minced
- ½ tsp onion powder
- 1 tsp paprika
- 1 ½ tsp salt
- ¾ tsp black pepper
- 1 ½ tsp cumin
- ½ tsp basil
- 1 ½ pounds chicken breasts cut into bit size pieces
- 1 large onion diced
- 1 red pepper diced
- 1 yellow or orange pepper diced
- 1 ½ tbsp coconut oil

Steps:

1. Mix oregano, chili powder, onion powder, garlic, paprika, salt, pepper, cumin, and basil in a small bowl. Mix well.
2. Add a tbsp of coconut oil to a saucepan and add the chicken and half of the spice mixer.

3. Stir frequently until the meat is cooked through (about 5-7 min). Put in a bowl or plate.
4. Add the rest of the oil, onion, and peppers to the pan. Spread the rest of the spice mixer on top and cook, about 8 to 10 minutes, until tender.
5. Serve the chicken, peppers, and onions over romaine lettuce or cauliflower rice and garnish with avocado if desired.

Per serving:

Calories: 332; Total Fat: 9.3g; Cholesterol: 131mg; Sodium: 101mg; Total Carbohydrate: 9.8g; Dietary Fiber: 2.8g; Total Sugars: 4.5g; Protein: 50.9g

---

91. Hemp Broiled Tilapia with Ginger

Preparation time: 4 Hours

Cooking Time: 10 Minutes

Servings: 8

What you need:

- 8 (6 ounces each) Tilapia fillets
- 1 cup coconut aminos
- 1 cup apple cider vinegar
- tbsp coconut oil
- tbsp fresh ginger, peeled and minced
- tsp garlic powder
- 1 cup leek finely chopped
- ½ cup Hemp Seeds

Steps:

1. In a large glass bowl, mix the coconut aminos, apple cider vinegar, coconut oil, garlic powder, ginger, and half the chopped leek.
2. Place the Tilapia in a large zippered bag, pour the marinade liquid into the bag, wring out any excess air, and seal it.
3. Marinate the Tilapia in the refrigerator for 2 to 4 hours.
4. Preheat the grill for 5 minutes. Take the fillets from the bag and place them skin side down on a baking sheet covered with a silicone baking mat. Sprinkle liberally with hemp seeds and pat firmly against the Tilapia. Tilapia should be completely covered with hemp seeds.
5. Place the pan on the top rack of your oven (or under the grill if you have a separate grill) and cook for 7-8 minutes, or until the fillets are flaky but still sag slightly when pressed
6. While the fillets are cooking, pour the remaining marinade into a saucepan and bring it to a boil. Then, simmer and reduce while the fillets are cooking.

7. Serve the Tilapia with the reduced marinade and garnish with the remaining leeks or herbs of your choice.

Per serving:

Calories: 250; Total Fat: 11.5g; Cholesterol: 55mg; Sodium: 79mg; Total Carbohydrate: 11g; Dietary Fiber: 0.9g; Total Sugars: 0.9g; Protein: 24.1g

---

92. Baked Chicken with Barley

Preparation time: 10 Minutes

Cooking Time: 10 Minutes

Servings: 8

What you need:

- 8 boneless, skinless chicken breasts (5 to 6 ounces each)
- 2cups barley (uncooked)
- 4 cups fat-free, low-sodium chicken broth
- 2 (14ounce) can dice tomatoes (undrained)
- 1 medium onion, chopped
- 1 cup carrot, sliced
- ½ cup green peas
- 1 tsp garlic powder
- 1 tsp dried basil
- 6 cups fresh baby kale, chopped

Steps:

1. Preheat the oven to 400 F.
2. Put the chicken breasts in a single layer in a baking dish that can accommodate the chicken in a single layer.
3. Mix uncooked barley, chicken broth, tomatoes, onions, carrot, green peas, garlic powder, and basil in a medium bowl.
4. Add the chopped kale.
5. Pour the mixture over the chicken.
6. Cover with foil and bake, 35-40 minutes, until the chicken is cooked through and the barley is tender.
7. Serve and Have a healthy meal!

Per serving:

Calories: 497; Total Fat: 11.5g; Cholesterol: 125mg; Sodium: 546mg; Total Carbohydrate: 48.5g; Dietary Fiber: 11.6g; Total Sugars: 5.7g; Protein: 49.9g

Tot time: 25 Minutes

Preparation time: 10 Minutes

Cooking Time: 15 Minutes

Makes: 3

What you need:

- 10-ounce grilled chicken breasts
- 3/4 cup brown rice
- 1 1/4 cup coconut water
- 1 teaspoon minced garlic
- 2 tablespoons teriyaki sauce
- 1 tablespoon extra-virgin olive oil
- 2 tablespoons cider vinegar
- 1 small red onion, chopped
- 5 radishes, sliced
- 1 cup broccoli, chopped
- Dash of sea salt

Steps:

1. Cook rice in coconut water following package instructions. Take from heat, let cool completely, and then fluff with a fork.
2. Whisk together garlic, teriyaki sauce, extra virgin olive oil, and vinegar. Stir in red onion, radishes, broccoli, and rice. Season with salt and stir until well mixed. Serve with grilled chicken breasts.

Per serving:

Calories: 242; Total Fat: 6.1g; Carbs: 41.8g; Dietary Fiber: 2.8g; Protein: 5.4g; Cholesterol: 0mg; Sodium: 554mg; sugars: 2.9g

---

94. Steamed Chicken with Mushroom and Ginger

Tot time: 20 Minutes

Preparation time: 10 Minutes

Cooking Time: 10 Minutes

Makes: 4

What you need:

- 4 x 150g chicken breast fillets
- 2 teaspoons extra-virgin olive oil

- 1 1/2 tablespoons balsamic vinegar
- 8cm piece ginger, cut into matchsticks
- 1 bunch broccoli
- 1 bunch carrots, diced
- 6 small dried shiitake mushrooms, chopped
- Spring onion, sliced
- Fresh coriander leaves,

Steps:

1. In a bowl, mix sliced chicken with salt, vinegar, and pepper; let marinate for at least 10 minutes.
2. Move the chicken to a baking dish and top with mushrooms and ginger; bake for about 15 minutes in a preheated oven at 350 °F; top with chopped broccoli and carrots and return to the oven. Cook for another 3 minutes or until chicken is tender.
3. Divide the chicken, broccoli, and carrots on serving plates and drizzle each with olive oil, and top with coriander and red onions. Have a healthy meal!

Per serving:

Calories: 242; Total Fat: 5 g; Carbs: 10 g; Dietary Fiber: 4 g; Sugars: 2 g; Protein: 37 g; Cholesterol: 88 mg; Sodium: 114 mg

---

95. Detox Salad with Grilled White Fish

Tot time: 10 Minutes

Preparation time: 10 Minutes

Cooking Time: N/A

Makes: 2

What you need:

For the Salad:

- 2 (150g each) pre-grilled white fish
- ½ cup snap peas, sliced
- 1 cup baby spinach
- 1 cup chopped Romaine lettuce
- ½ cup avocado, sliced
- ½ cup blueberries
- 2 green onions, sliced
- ½ cup shredded carrot
- 1 large cucumber, chopped
- 1 tablespoon chia seeds

For the Dressing:

- 1 clove garlic, minced
- ¼ teaspoon oregano
- 1 tablespoon tahini
- 1 teaspoon honey
- 1 tablespoon rice wine vinegar
- 1/8 teaspoon red pepper flakes
- 1 tablespoon lemon juice
- ¼ teaspoon black pepper
- 1 teaspoon sesame oil
- ¼ teaspoon salt

Steps:

1. Mix all salad ingredients, except the fish, in a large mixing bowl. Whisk together all dressing ingredients in a small bowl until thoroughly mixd; pour over salad and toss until well mixd.
2. Enjoy the grilled white fish on top of each plate!

Per serving:

Calories: 256; Total Fat: 14.1 g; Carbs: 29.7 g; Cholesterol: 0 mg; Dietary Fiber: 8.5 g; Sugars: 13.5 g; Protein: 6.5 g; Sodium: 343 mg

---

96. Yummy Egg Salad with Olives

Tot time: 30 Minutes

Preparation time: 10 Minutes

Cooking Time: 20 Minutes

Makes: 2

What you need:

Salad:

- 2 free-range eggs
- 2 potatoes, washed
- 1 cup prepared green beans
- 1 red onion, sliced
- 7 cherry tomatoes, cut in half
- 6 lettuce leaves, torn
- 5 kalamata olives, pitted and chopped

Dressing:

- 2 tablespoons rapeseed oil
- 1 tablespoon water
- 1 teaspoon balsamic vinegar
- 1 clove garlic, minced

- 2 kalamata olives, pitted and finely chopped
- Juice of 1 lemon
- 1/3 cup freshly chopped basil

Steps:

1. Add all the dressing ingredients in a bowl and mix until well mixd, then set aside.
2. Place the potatoes in a small saucepan with water and salt and bring to a boil and cook for about 6 minutes. Add in the beans and cook for 5 minutes. Meanwhile, boil the eggs for 8 minutes, set in cold water, then peel.
3. Peel the potatoes, chop them, add them to a large bowl, and mix them with the green beans and all other salad ingredients apart from the eggs. Drizzle in half the dressing in the potato mixture and mix well.
4. Cut the eggs diagonally and arrange them on top of the salad. Drizzle with the remaining dressing.
5. Serve immediately.

Per serving:

Calories: 344; Total Fat: 31.9 g; Net Carbs: 2.3 g; Dietary Fiber: 1.3g; Sugars: 4.1; Protein: 13 g; Cholesterol: 0 mg; Sodium: 350.6 mg

---

97. Yummy Chicken and Sweet Potato Stew

Tot time: 4-8 Hours

Preparation time: 15 Minutes

Cooking Time: 4-8 Hours

Makes: 4-6

What you need:

- 1-pound boneless chicken breasts, with skin, removed and cut into chunks
- 4 cloves garlic, crushed
- 1 Vidalia onion, chopped
- 1 sweet potato, peeled and cut into cubes
- 3 carrots, peeled and diced
- 3 tablespoons balsamic vinegar
- 2 cups of chicken broth
- 2 cups fresh baby spinach
- 2-4 tablespoons tomato paste
- 2 teaspoons whole grain mustard
- Freshly ground pepper and salt to taste

Steps:

1. In your slow cooker, mix all of the ingredients and stir well until equally mixed.

2. Cook on low for 6 to 8 hours or high for 4-5 hours, covered.
3. Stir in the baby spinach when there are only a few minutes left in the cooking time.
4. Serve immediately.

Per serving:

Calories: 139 Total Fat: 11.7g; Net Carbs: 2.6 g; Dietary Fiber: 3.8 g; Protein: 5.4 g Sugars: 1.2 g; Sodium: 224mg;

---

98. Asparagus Quinoa & Steak Bowl

Tot time: 25 Minutes

Preparation time: 10

Cooking Time: 15 Minutes

Makes: 4

What you need:

- 1-1/2 cups white quinoa
- Olive oil cooking spray
- 3/4 pound beef top sirloin steak, diced
- 1/2 tsp. low-sodium steak seasoning
- 1/2 cup chopped red bell pepper
- 1/2 cup chopped red onion
- 1 cup frozen asparagus cuts
- 2 ½ tbsp. soy sauce
- 1 avocado, sliced

Steps:

1. Follow package instructions to cook quinoa.
2. Meantime, coat a large skillet with cooking spray and heat over medium-high heat.
3. Sprinkle beef with the steak seasoning and cook in the skillet for about 3 minutes; add bell pepper and red onion and cook for 3 minutes more or until beef is browned. Add asparagus and continue cooking for 4 minutes or until asparagus is heated through.
4. Stir soy sauce to the quinoa until well mixd, and toss it with the beef mixture before serving with avocado.

Per serving:

Calories: 325; Total Fat: 38.2 g; Carbs: 17.4 g; Dietary Fiber: 11.1 g; Sugars: 6.2 g; Protein: 26.3 g; Cholesterol: 121 mg; Sodium: 984 mg

Tot time: 20 Minutes

Preparation time: 10 Minutes

Cooking Time: 10 Minutes

Makes: 8

What you need:

- 1/2 cup frozen pea
- 2 cups cooked brown rice
- 2 tablespoons extra-virgin olive oil
- 1 red chili, sliced
- 2 garlic cloves, sliced
- 1 red onion, sliced
- 1 cup large peeled prawn
- 1 bunch coriander, chopped
- 1 tablespoon fish sauce
- 1 tablespoon dark soy sauce
- 4 large eggs
- 1 tablespoon chili sauce

Steps:

1. Sauté garlic, onion, and chili in hot oil in a skillet for about 3 minutes or until golden; stir in prawns for about 1 minute and then toss in peas and rice. Cook until heated through. Stir in fish sauce, soy sauce, and coriander and cook for a minute.
2. Remove from heat and keep warm.
3. Heat oil in a pan and fry the eggs; season.
4. Divide the rice mixture among four serving plates and top each with a fried egg. Serve with chili sauce topped with coriander.

Per serving:

Calories: 278; Total Fat: 7.3 g; Carbs: 44.9 g; Dietary Fiber: 3 g; Sugars: 5.4 g; Protein: 8.3 g; Cholesterol: 95 mg; Sodium: 1096 mg

---

100.   Curried Prawns with Whole-Wheat Bread

Tot time: 1 Hour

Preparation time: 15 Minutes

Cooking Time: 25 Minutes

Makes: 4

What you need:

- 7.9-ounce jumbo prawns, peeled
- 2.6-ounce baby corn, cut in half
- 1 cup vegetable stock
- 1-inch ginger root, thinly stripped
- 2 teaspoons desiccated coconut
- 1 red chili, seeded and thinly sliced
- 1 can coconut milk
- 2 tablespoons hot curry powder
- 2.6-ounces sugar snap peas
- 1 large sweet potato, cubed
- Juice of 1 lime
- ½ cup thinly sliced spring onions for serving
- Salt and pepper to taste

Steps:

1. Toast the coconut in a large pan for about 2 minutes until it turns golden. Transfer into a bowl. Return the pan to heat, add curry powder, and toast it until fragrant for about a minute then add in the sweet potato cubes, chili, and ginger.
2. Pour in the stock and coconut milk and bring to a boil. Turn the heat to low and simmer for 10 minutes until the potatoes are tender.
3. Stir in the veggies and cook for 5 minutes until soft. Next, add the prawns and cook for about 2 minutes or until they turn pink. Season the curry.
4. Turn off the heat and stir in the spring onions and lime juice.
5. Serve with whole-wheat bread and top with toasted coconut

Per serving:

Calories: 367; Total Fat: 16.5 g; Net Carbs: 31.6 g; Dietary Fiber:1.9 g; Protein: 26 g; Sugar: 13 g; Sodium: 1198 mg; Cholesterol: 112 mg

---

101.   Healthy Creamy Chicken Salsa

Tot time: 40Minutes

Preparation time: 10 Minutes

Cooking Time: 30 Minutes

Makes: 2

What you need:

- 1 chicken breast, cut in half
- 4 tablespoons cheddar cheese
- 1 tablespoon unsweetened Greek yogurt
- 2 teaspoons, taco seasoning mix
- ½ cup organic salsa

Steps:

1. Now at first preheat your oven to 375 degrees F and prepare a baking dish by lightly coating it with coconut oil or olive oil.
2. Generously season the chicken breasts with taco seasoning, the arrangement on the baking dish, and the salsa.
3. Bake for half an hour or until the chicken is done to desire. Sprinkle with cheese and put back in the oven until the cheese melts.
4. Serve hot with Greek yogurt.

Per serving:

Calories: 287; Total Fat: 10.4 g; Net Carbs: 5.7 g; Dietary Fiber: 2.5; Sugars: 0.4; Protein: 21.8 g; Cholesterol: 0 mg; Sodium: 864 mg

---

102.   Italian Chicken Balls with Green Salad

Tot time: 40Minutes

Preparation time: 20 Minutes

Cooking Time: 20 Minutes

Makes: 4

What you need:

- 15-ounce ground chicken
- 1 tablespoon garlic powder
- 1 tablespoon Italian seasoning
- 2 eggs
- ¼ cup coconut yogurt
- 2 tablespoons coconut yogurt
- 1 teaspoon salt
- 1 teaspoon freshly ground black pepper
- 1 tablespoon panko crumbs
- 1 teaspoon red pepper flakes

Steps:

1. At first preheat the oven to 450 °F. Coat a baking pan with aluminum foil and coconut oil.

2. In a large mixing basin, add all of the ingredients and stir well to incorporate. Make chicken balls of uniform size and place them on the prepared sheet.
3. Bake for about 20 minutes until golden and cooked.
4. Serve hot with your favorite salad.

Per serving:

Calories: 164; Total Fat: 7.3 g; Net Carbs: 3.2 g; Dietary Fiber: 1.1g; Sugars: 0.5; Protein: 17.9 g; Cholesterol: 0 mg; Sodium: 299 mg

---

103.   Tasty Vegan Steaks

Tot time: 60Minutes

Preparation time: 15 Minutes

Cooking Time: 45 Minutes

Makes: 6

What you need:

- 1 head green cabbage
- 3 garlic cloves, minced
- 2 tablespoons extra virgin olive oil
- ½ teaspoon sea salt
- ½ teaspoon freshly ground black pepper

Steps:

1. At first preheat your oven to 350 degrees F. Cut the cabbage into thick slices and arrange them on a casserole dish.
2. Drizzle olive oil over the cabbage and sprinkle with garlic. Sprinkle some pepper and salt as per taste and cover with aluminum foil.
3. Bake for 45 minutes. Serve warm. Have a healthy meal!

Per serving:

Calories: 81; Total Fat: 4.7 g; Net Carbs: 8.4 g; Dietary Fiber: 9.1g; Sugars: 1.1; Protein: 2.7 g; Cholesterol: 0 mg; Sodium: 221 mg

---

104.   Classic Spaghetti with Meatballs

Tot time: 55Minutes

Preparation time: 20 Minutes

Cooking Time: 35 Minutes

Makes: 4

What you need:

- ¼ cup mozzarella
- 1 packet spaghetti
- 1 cup organic pasta sauce
- 1 tablespoon extra-virgin olive oil
- 12 Italian chicken meatballs (check earlier recipe)

Steps:

1. Preheat your oven to 375 degrees F. Grease a 6 cup muffin pan with olive oil.
2. According to package instructions, cook spaghetti, drain and put in the fridge to cool for 15 minutes.
3. Mix the cheese with the spaghetti from the fridge, then divide it up in the greased muffin pan, creating a small nest for the meatballs.
4. Add a tablespoon of pasta sauce, followed by a meatball and more pasta sauce. If you have any leftover cheese sprinkle it on top, then bake for 20 minutes.
5. Serve hot and Have a healthy meal!

Per serving:

Calories: 402; Total Fat: 11.3 g; Net Carbs: 41.2 g; Dietary Fiber: 1.3g; Sugars: 2.1; Protein: 26 g; Cholesterol: 0 mg; Sodium: 635 mg

---

105.   Jerk Chicken & Brown Rice

Tot time: 1 Hour

Preparation time: 15 Minutes

Cooking Time: 45 Minutes

Makes: 6

What you need:

For the chicken:

- 6 chicken thighs
- 2 tablespoons jerk seasoning
- ½ teaspoon chicken seasoning

For the rice:

- 2 cups brown rice
- 4 tablespoons olive oil
- 1 red onion, chopped
- 2 bay leaves
- 4 garlic cloves, minced

- 1 large can of coconut oil
- 2 ½ cups chicken broth
- 1 scotch bonnet
- 2 teaspoons jerk seasoning
- 1 teaspoon sweet paprika
- Salt and pepper to taste
- 1 teaspoon dried thyme
- 1/3 cup finely sliced green onions

Steps:

1. Preheat oven to 350 degrees F.
2. Make slits on chicken thighs and rub with jerk seasoning salt and chicken spice.
3. Add half the oil to a Dutch oven, brown the chicken for 3 minutes per side, and then set aside.
4. Remove any burnt pieces from the Dutch oven, add the remaining oil, and stir in the onions. Bay leaves garlic and thyme and cook for about 3 minutes. Stir in the rice and beans for a minute and pour in all the remaining ingredients apart from the green onions.
5. Put the Dutch oven in the preheated oven and cook for about 35 minutes or until the chicken and rice are perfectly cooked.
6. Take out from oven and garnish with green onions.

Per serving:

Calories: 503; Total Fat: 28.7 g; Net Carbs: 37.8 g; Dietary Fiber: 2.9 g; Sugars: 2 g; Protein: 21.2 g; Cholesterol: 71 mg; Sodium: 335 mg

---

106.   Delicious Buckwheat with Mushrooms & Green Onions

Tot time: 55 Minutes

Preparation time: 20 Minutes

Cooking Time: 35 Minutes

Makes: 6

What you need:

- 1 cup uncooked buckwheat
- 2 cup water
- 2 cups mushrooms
- 1 red onion, chopped
- 1 cup chopped green onions
- 3 tablespoons butter

- A pinch of salt and pepper

Steps:

1. Mix buckwheat, salt, and water in a pan, bring to a boil, cook for 25 minutes or until liquid is absorbed.
2. Melt butter in a pan and fry in red onion until tender; stir in mushrooms and cook for 5 minutes or until golden brown. Stir in cooked buckwheat and remove from heat. Serve topped with freshly chopped green onions.

Per serving:

Calories: 166; Total Fat: 6.8 g; Net Carbs: 20.1 g; Dietary Fiber: 3.9 g; Sugars: 1.6; Protein: 5.1 g; Cholesterol: 15 mg; Sodium: 48 mg

---

107.   Healthy Fish Curry with Brown Rice

Tot time: 30 Minutes

Preparation time: 10 Minutes

Cooking Time: 20 Minutes

Makes: 4

What you need:

- 4 skinless white fish fillets
- 2 tablespoons fresh juice
- 2 tablespoons curry powder
- 1 tablespoon groundnut oil
- 1 cup sliced spring onions
- 2-inch ginger root, grated
- 2 cloves garlic, crushed
- 1 scotch bonnet chili, chopped
- 1 red pepper, chopped
- 1 teaspoon chopped thyme
- 2 cups coconut milk
- 4 cups steamed brown rice

Steps:

1. Mix lemon juice and half of the Caribbean curry powder and rub onto the fish; let sit for a few minutes.
2. Heat oil in a pan and cook onion, garlic, chili, ginger, and pepper for about 5 minutes. Stir in thyme and the remaining curry powder for about 1 minute. Add coconut milk and simmer for about 10 minutes or until the sauce is thick.
3. Add in the fish and simmer, covered, for about 10 minutes or until the fish is cooked through.

4. Serve over cooked rice topped with fresh thyme.

Per serving:

Calories: 314; Total Fat: 21 g; Net Carbs: 4 g; Dietary Fiber: 3 g; Sugar: 4 g; Protein: 29 g; Sodium: 400 mg; Cholesterol: 0 mg

---

108.   Beef & Sweet Potato Enchilada Casserole

Tot time: 40 Minutes

Preparation time: 20 Minutes

Cooking Time: 20 Minutes

Makes: 10

What you need:

- 2 sweet potatoes
- 1 pound ground beef
- 1 can black beans, drained
- 1 cup frozen corn
- 1 can red enchilada sauce
- 4 tablespoon chopped fresh cilantro
- 2 teaspoon ground cumin
- 1 teaspoon garlic powder
- 1 teaspoon onion powder
- 12 corn tortillas
- 1 small can diced olives
- 1 cup shredded parmesan cheese

Steps:

1. Peel and cook the sweet potatoes; mash and mix with 2 tablespoons of cilantro.
2. Cook the ground beef and then stir in beans, corn, sauce, and spices until well mixd.
3. Layer half of the meat mixture in a 9x13-inch pan and top with half corn tortilla; sprinkle with half of the cheese and repeat the layers.
4. Top with sweet potatoes, olives, and cilantro. Cover the remaining cheese and bake at 350°F for about 25 minutes or until cheese is melted.

Per serving:

Calories: 315; Total Fat: 8.2 g; Net Carbs: 5.4 g; Dietary Fiber: 12.5 g; Sugars: 3.2 g; Protein: 31.6 g; Cholesterol: 54 mg; Sodium: 172 mg

Tot time: 45 Minutes

Preparation time: 10 Minutes

Cooking Time: 35 Minutes

Makes: 4

What you need:

- 4 (140g each) salmon fillets
- 1 bunch asparagus, trimmed
- 3 cups baby potatoes, diced
- 9 oz. cherry tomatoes, diced
- 8 sprigs of fresh lemon thyme
- 1 tablespoon extra-virgin olive oil
- 2 lemons, plus lemon zest to serve
- 1/4 teaspoon cracked pepper

Steps:

1. Turn the oven to 400°F for preheat and prepare a baking sheet with parchment paper. Toss together the lemon juice, potatoes, half of the thyme, lemon wedges, and two tablespoons of oil on the prepared tray until evenly coated.
2. Roast for approximately 15 minutes, then add the tomatoes; cook for another 10 minutes; arrange the asparagus and salmon on top of the vegetables and sprinkle with the remaining oil.
3. Continue to roast for an additional 8 minutes. Serve with lemon zest and thyme on top. Have a healthy meal!

Per serving:

Calories: 416; Total Fat: 19.7 g; Carbs: 20.2 g; Dietary Fiber: 6.6 g; Sugars: 2.3 g; Protein: 34.1 g; Cholesterol: 68 mg; Sodium: 112 mg

Tot time: 40 Minutes

Preparation time: 15 Minutes

Cooking Time: 25 Minutes

Makes: 4

What you need:

- 2/3 cup black rice
- 2 (200g each) chicken breast fillets
- 2 cups chopped broccoli
- 7.1-ounce snap peas, trimmed
- 1 1/2 cups picked watercress leaves
- 1 1/2 tablespoon salt-reduced tamari
- 1 tablespoon sesame seeds
- 2 tablespoons tahini
- 1/2 teaspoon raw honey

Steps:

1. Boil rice in a saucepan for about 15 minutes or until al dente; drain. Coat chicken fillets with sesame seeds and cook in hot oil in a skillet set over medium-high heat for 5 minutes per side or until cooked through.
2. Let cool and slice. In the meantime, steam broccoli and peas until tender. In a small bowl, whisk tahini, tamari, and raw honey until very smooth. Divide cooked black rice among serving bowls and top each with broccoli and peas.
3. Top with chicken and watercress; drizzle each serving with tahini dressing. Have a healthy meal!

Per serving:

Calories: 325; Total Fat: 6 g; Carbs: 26 g; Dietary Fiber: 9 g; Sugars: 11 g; Protein: 35 g; Cholesterol: 94 mg; Sodium: 210 mg

---

111.   Crunchy Watercress Sandwich

Tot time: 30 Minutes

Preparation time: 10 Minutes

Cooking Time: 20 Minutes

Makes: 4

What you need:

- 8 free-range eggs
- 4 green onions, sliced
- 4 tablespoons unsweetened Greek yogurt
- ¾ cup watercress, stems removed and cleaned
- 1 tablespoon Dijon mustard
- Salt and black pepper to taste
- 8 slice wholemeal bread

Steps:

1. Boil the eggs for 8-10 eggs. Remove from heat, put in a bowl of cold water for about a minute or two, then peel, cut in half, and set aside. Separate the yolks from the whites and chop all the whites. Mash two yolks in a small bowl and mix the Greek yogurt and Dijon mustard.
2. Mix the chopped egg whites with the onions and season with salt and pepper. Roughly chop the remaining yolks and add to the egg white mix. Mix in the yogurt mix and mix well.
3. Set out four slices of bread and top with watercress leaves, egg salad. Cover with the remaining slices. Slice diagonally and Have a healthy meal!

Per serving:

Calories: 158; Total Fat: 10.1 g; Net Carbs: 13.3 g; Dietary Fiber: 2.8g; Sugars: 4.1; Protein: 6.2 g; Cholesterol: 0 mg; Sodium: 317 mg

---

112.   Tangy Fillets with Sweet Potato Flakes

Tot time: 30 Minutes

Preparation time: 20 Minutes

Cooking Time: 10 Minutes

Makes: 4

What you need:

- 1 free-range egg
- 1 ½ cups shaved/ grated sweet potato
- ¼ cup coconut oil
- 2 tablespoons Dijon mustard
- 4 white fish fillets
- Salt and black pepper to taste

Steps:

1. Mix the egg, Dijon, salt, and pepper in a shallow bowl. Put the shaved sweet potato in a separate shallow bowl. Heat the coconut oil in a heavy-bottomed pan.
2. Meanwhile, dip the fillets in the egg mix, then dredge them in the sweet potato shavings. Dip the fish a second time in the two bowls for a very crisp coating. Fry the fillets for 3-5 minutes per side or until golden and crisp.
3. Serve hot with your salad of choice.

Per serving:

Calories: 199; Total Fat: 12.5 g; Net Carbs: 8.7 g; Dietary Fiber: 1.9g; Sugars: 2.2; Protein: 16.6 g; Cholesterol: 0 mg; Sodium: 714.9 mg

Tot time: 65 Minutes

Preparation time: 15 Minutes

Cooking Time: 50 Minutes

Makes: 4

What you need:

- 1 package egg noodles
- 1 cup almond milk
- ¼ cup sharp cheddar cheese, shredded
- 2 tablespoon coconut oil
- 1 can tuna, drained
- 2 tablespoons almond flour
- 1 can peas, drained and rinsed
- Salt, to taste

Steps:

1. Turn the oven to 350°F for preheat and grease a casserole dish with coconut or olive oil. Cook the noodles as per box directions, then drain and set aside. In a small non-stick pan, mix the coconut oil, almond flour, and salt until well mixd, then whisk in the almond milk until you have a thick sauce.
2. Stir in the shredded cheese, peas, noodles, and tuna.
3. Remove from heat and transfer to the prepared casserole dish and bake in the preheated oven for half an hour. Serve hot.

Per serving:

Calories: 346; Total Fat: 14.6 g; Net Carbs: 28.2 g; Dietary Fiber: 3.1g; Sugars: 0.9; Protein: 19.3 g; Cholesterol: 0 mg; Sodium: 721 mg

---

114.   Cheesy Tortilla Casserole

Tot time: 35 Minutes

Preparation time: 15 Minutes

Cooking Time: 20 Minutes

Makes: 2

What you need:

- I cup organic salsa
- 2 tablespoons olive oil
- ½ can refried beans

- 1 sweet onion, diced
- ½ cup ricotta cheese
- 3 gluten-free tortillas

Directions

1. Start by preheating your oven to 375 degrees F. Coat a non-stick pan with olive oil.
2. Cook the onions in a pan over medium heat until soft and add in the refried beans and cook for 5 minutes. Spread a tortilla at the base of the prepared pan and spread one-third of the bean mixture, followed by the salsa and the cheese. Repeat with the remaining tortillas, beans, salsa, and cheese.
3. Bake for 15 minutes or until the cheese melts beautifully.

Per serving:

Calories: 302; Total Fat: 13.4 g; Net Carbs: 22.1 g; Dietary Fiber: 2.6g; Sugars: 1.3; Protein: 20.1 g; Cholesterol: 0 mg; Sodium: 567 mg

---

115.   *Healthy Chicken & Veggies with Toasted Walnuts*

Tot time: 25 Minutes

Preparation time: 10 Minutes

Cooking Time: 15 Minutes

Makes: 4

What you need:

- 4 (about 250g) chicken tenderloins
- 1 teaspoon extra virgin olive oil
- 1 small zucchini, sliced
- 1/4 cup of pitted and halved green olives
- 2 cups drained and rinsed cannellini beans
- 1 cup chopped green beans
- 1 tablespoon fresh lemon juice
- 2 garlic cloves, sliced
- 15 ounce can cherry tomatoes
- 1 teaspoon harissa paste
- 1 teaspoon smoked paprika
- Fresh parsley sprigs
- 1 cup toasted walnuts, chopped

Steps:

1. In a plastic container, mix together lemon juice, garlic, harissa, and paprika until well mixd; add in chicken and shake to coat well. Let sit for a few minutes.
2. In a pan, heat the oil and add the chicken, along with the marinade; cook for about 2 minutes per side, or until golden brown. Stir in the veggies and simmer

for about 10 minutes or until tender. Divide on serving plates and serve topped with fresh parsley and toasted walnuts.

Per serving:

Calories: 129; Total Fat: 11 g; Carbs: 23 g; Dietary Fiber: 13.5g; Sugars: 2.3 g; Protein: 41 g; Cholesterol: 123 mg; Sodium: 114 mg

---

116.   Mixed Green Salad w/ Sage & Chile-Roasted Acorn Squash

---

Tot time: 5 Minutes

Preparation time: 5 Minutes

Cooking Time: N/A

Makes: 4

What you need:

- 2 tart apples, cut into matchsticks
- 2 acorn squash, roasted
- Pinch of sea salt
- Pinch of pepper
- 2-3 tablespoons olive oil
- ¼ cup fresh lemon juice

Steps:

1. Place lettuce leaf in a salad bowl and top with apple slices and squash; sprinkle with pepper and salt and drizzle with olive oil and fresh lemon juice; toss and serve right away.

Per serving:

Calories: 208; Total Fat: 7.5 g; Net Carbs: 32.2 g; Dietary Fiber: 6 g; Sugars: 11.9 g; Protein: 2.1 g; Cholesterol: 0 mg; Sodium: 69 mg

---

117.   Healthy Millet Lettuce Wraps

Tot time: 30 Minutes

Preparation time: 10 Minutes

Cooking Time: 20 Minutes

Makes: 2

What you need:

- 4 leaves lettuce

- ¼ cup millet
- 1 teaspoon butter
- ½ cup water
- ¼ red onion, chopped
- 1 clove garlic, minced
- 2 tablespoons fresh lime juice
- 1 teaspoon chopped cilantro
- ½ teaspoon sea salt
- 1 carrot, chopped

Steps:

1. In a skillet, toast millet for about 5 minutes or until fragrant and toasted; transfer to a plate and set aside. Add butter to the skillet and sauté in red onion and garlic for about 3 minutes or until fragrant.
2. Stir in toasted millet, lime juice, cilantro, sea salt, and water; simmer for about 10 minutes or until the liquid is absorbed. Remove from heat.
3. Divide carrots among the lettuce leave and top each with the millet mixture. Roll to form wraps and serve.

Per serving:

Calories: 133; Total Fat: 3 g; Net Carbs: 19.9 g; Dietary Fiber: 3.3 g; Sugars: 2.2; Protein: 3.3 g; Cholesterol: 5 mg; Sodium: 507 mg

---

118.   Millet Stir Fry with Veggies

Tot time: 30 Minutes

Preparation time: 20 Minutes

Cooking Time: 20 Minutes

Makes: 2

What you need:

- 1 cup millet
- 1 red onion, chopped
- 1 green chili, chopped
- 1 tablespoon grated ginger
- 2 cloves garlic, minced
- 1/2 cup chopped red and green bell peppers
- 1/2 cup chopped French beans
- 1/2 cup chopped carrots
- 1 teaspoon coriander powder
- 1 teaspoon cumin powder

- 1 teaspoon turmeric powder
- Salt to taste
- 1 tablespoon olive oil
- fresh coriander leaves

Steps:

1. Wash millet under running water and soak for at least 10 minutes.
2. Meanwhile, heat oil in a pot and cook in garlic, ginger, and green chili for 1 minute; stir in onions and spices and cook for 2 minutes.
3. Rinse the millet and drain; add to the pot along with two cups of water. Cover and cook for 10 minutes or until liquid is absorbed and millet is tender. Fluff and serve topped with fresh coriander.

Per serving:

Calories: 327; Total Fat: 6.4 g; Net Carbs: 35.8 g; Dietary Fiber: 11.7 g; Sugars: 2 g Protein: 10.7g; Cholesterol: 0 mg; Sodium: 58 mg

---

119.   Warm Bean Soup with Whole-Wheat Tortilla Chips

Tot time: 1 Hour 10 Minutes

Preparation time: 10 Minutes

Cooking Time: 1 Hour

Makes: 6

What you need:

- 6 cups boiling water
- 1 large red onion, diced
- 1 pound dried black beans
- 1/4 teaspoon chipotle chile powder
- 2 teaspoons cumin
- 1 teaspoon sea salt
- 1 cup salsa
- 12 ounces frozen corn kernels
- 1 tablespoon fresh lime juice
- Avocado slices
- baked Whole-wheat tortilla chips

Steps:

1. Boil water in an instant pot and turn it to sauté setting; add onion and cook, often stirring, until tender and browned.

2. Stir in beans, chipotle chili powder, cumin, boiling water, and sea salt; turn off the sauté function. Lock lid in place and turn on high pressure, adjusting time to 30 minutes. Let the pressure come down naturally before opening the pot.
3. Remove about 3 cups of beans to a mixer and mix until very smooth; return to pot and add salsa and corn. Adjust seasoning and turn the pot on sauté; cook until heated through. Ladle in serving bowls and drizzle with lime juice, garnish with avocado slices, and serve with baked tortilla chips.

Per serving:

Calories: 329; Total Fat: 1 g; Carbs: 65 g; Dietary Fiber: 15 g; Sugars: 7 g; Protein: 18 g; Cholesterol: 0 mg; Sodium: 707 mg

---

120.   Avocado-Kale Salad with Grilled Lime Steak

Tot time: 10 Minutes

Preparation time: 10 Minutes

Cooking Time: N/A

Makes: 6

What you need:

For the salad:

- 1 kg lean steak
- ¼ cup freshly squeezed lime juice
- A pinch of sea salt
- A pinch of pepper
- 2 large carrots, grated
- 1 red bell pepper, cut into matchsticks
- 2 cups broccoli florets
- 2 cups thinly sliced red cabbage
- 2 cups kale, thinly sliced
- 1 cup walnuts
- 2 avocados, diced
- 1/2 cup chopped parsley
- 1 tablespoon sesame seeds

For the dressing:

- 1/2 cup lemon juice, fresh
- 1/3 cup grapeseed oil
- 2 teaspoons whole grain mustard
- 1 tablespoon grated fresh ginger
- 1/4 teaspoon sea salt

- 1 teaspoon raw honey

Steps:

1. Mix lime juice, pepper, and salt in a small dish; sprinkle over the steak and grill for about 8 minutes each side, or until cooked to your preference, over a prepared charcoal grill.
2. Whisk all of the dressing ingredients in a small dish until thoroughly mixd; put aside.
3. Toss carrots, bell pepper, broccoli, cabbage, and greens in a large mixing basin with the dressing until completely covered. Toss in the walnuts, avocado, parsley, and sesame seeds to mix. Serve with the cooked steak on top and Have a healthy meal!

Per serving:

Calories: 332; Total Fat: 26.6 g; Carbs: 20.2 g; Cholesterol: 0 mg; Sodium: 138 mg Dietary Fiber: 9 g; Sugars: 5.5 g; Protein: 3.1 g;

---

121.   Lemon Grilled Salmon & Avocado Vegetable Salad

Tot time: 10 Minutes

Preparation time: 10 Minutes

Cooking Time: N/A

Makes: 8

Ingredients

- 3 (150g each) salmon fillet
- ¼ cup freshly squeezed lemon juice
- A pinch of sea salt
- A pinch of pepper
- 1 cup watercress, rinsed
- 1 zucchini, shaved
- 1 small red onion, sliced into thin rings
- 1 small broccoli head, rinsed and cut in small florets
- 1 avocado, diced
- 2 tablespoons s fresh lemon juice
- 1 tablespoon extra-virgin olive oil
- ½ teaspoon Dijon mustard
- ½ teaspoon sea salt
- ¼ cup crushed toasted almonds.
- 1 tablespoon chia seeds

Steps:

1. In a bowl, mix lemon juice, salt, and pepper until well mixd; smear on the fish fillets until well coated and grill on a preheated charcoal grill for about 7 minutes each side or until cooked and browned.
2. In another bowl, mix together the veggies until well mixd.
3. Whisk together the lemon juice, olive oil, mustard, and salt in a small bowl until thoroughly mixd; pour over the salad and toss to coat. Toss in the almonds and chia seeds to mix. Before serving, let the salad aside for at least 5 minutes to allow the flavors to meld.
4. Serve the salad drizzled with the dressing and topped with the grilled salmon for a healthy, satisfying meal.

Per serving:

Calories: 258; Total Fat: 22.1 g; Carbs: 14.1 g; Dietary Fiber: 7.7 g; Sugars: 3.5 g; Protein: 5.3 g; Cholesterol: 0 mg; Sodium: 352 mg

---

122.   Jamaican Curried Goat Pot

Tot time: 2 Hours

Preparation time: 15 Minutes

Cooking Time: 1 Hour 45 Minutes

Makes: 8

What you need:

- 2 pounds goat stew meat, diced
- 2 hot chile peppers, chopped
- 2 tablespoons curry powder
- 2 cloves garlic, minced
- 1 teaspoon salt
- 1 teaspoon black pepper
- 3 tablespoons olive oil
- 1 onion, chopped
- 1 rib celery, chopped
- 2 ½ cups vegetable broth
- 1 bay leaf
- 3 sweet potatoes, peeled, diced

Steps:

1. In a bowl, mix goat meat, garlic, chile pepper, curry powder, sea salt, and black pepper; refrigerate and cover for about 1 hour.
2. Now heat oil in a skillet over medium-high heat; remove meat from the marinade and fry in the hot oil for about 6 minutes; transfer to a plate and add

onion and celery to the skillet. Cook for about 6 minutes. Move the meat to the skillet and stir in vegetable broth, marinade, and bay leaf.
3. Bring to a gentle boil and then simmer for about 1 hour. Stir in potatoes and cook for another 35 minutes or until potatoes are tender.
4. Remove bay leaf and serve hot.

Per serving:

Calories: 239; Total Fat: 19.6 g; Net Carbs: 16.4 g; Dietary Fiber: 3.4 g; Sugars: 2 g; Protein: 22 g; Cholesterol: 66 mg; Sodium: 321 mg

---

123.   Black Bean & Oxtail Stew

Tot time: 2 Hours 10Minutes

Preparation time: 10 Minutes

Cooking Time: 2 Hours

Makes: 6

What you need:
- 2-pound oxtail cut up into large chunks
- 6 pimento seeds
- 3 tablespoons olive oil
- 1 scotch bonnet
- 1 red onion, chopped
- 4 garlic cloves, minced
- ½ teaspoon sweet paprika
- 1 tablespoon fresh thyme, finely chopped
- 1 tablespoon tomato paste
- 1 tablespoon Worcestershire sauce
- 1 cup black beans
- 1 teaspoon hot curry powder
- ½ cup green onions, for serving
- Salt and pepper to taste

Steps:
1. Season the oxtail well with salt and pepper.
2. Add oil to a large pot over medium heat. Once the pan is sizzling hot, add the oxtail and brown on all sides for about 5 minutes; if the oil is too much, drain and leave about 2 tablespoons.
3. Add all the remaining ingredients apart from the beans and green onions and cook for 2 minutes, stirring the whole time. Add 5 cups of water, bring to a boil, and then simmer for about 2 hours.
4. Add the beans and check for seasoning with the 20 minutes of cook time left.

5. Once ready, season with green onion and serve.

Per serving:

Calories: 570; Total Fat: 27.8 g; Net Carbs: 19.3 g; Dietary Fiber: 5.2 g; Sugars: 8.7 g; Protein: 22.3 g; Cholesterol: 167 mg; Sodium: 330 mg

---

124. *Spiced Grilled Chicken with Detox Salad & Mango Salsa*

Tot time: 17 Minutes

Preparation time: 5 Minutes

Cooking Time: 12 Minutes

Makes: 8

What you need:

- 1 teaspoon extra virgin olive oil
- 1 tablespoon ground coriander
- 1 garlic clove, crushed
- 1 teaspoon crushed dried chili
- 1 tablespoon smoked paprika
- 2 tablespoons ground cumin
- 4 (159 gram each) chicken breasts, boneless, skinless
- 1 teaspoon red pepper flakes
- 1 teaspoon graham masala

For the salad:

- 1 cup diced carrots
- 1 tablespoon rapeseed oil
- 1 cup halved cherry tomatoes
- 1 cup chopped red bell peppers
- 1 cup chopped yellow bell peppers
- 1 cup chopped spinach
- 1 cup grated beets
- 1/4 red onion, roughly diced
- A handful of fresh parsley
- A handful of fresh coriander
- A handful of fresh mint
- 2 avocados, sliced

For the mango salsa:

- 4 cherry tomatoes, diced
- 1 mango, diced
- 1 fresh red chili, seeded and chopped

- Juice of 1 lime
- Black pepper
- A handful of fresh coriander, finely chopped
- Sea salt

Steps:

1. To make the marinade, mix extra virgin olive oil, garlic, all spices, and salt in a large mixing bowl. Turn the chicken in the marinade until fully coated.
2. Melt butter in a grill pan or griddle over medium heat.
3. Meanwhile, working one at a time, place the chicken breasts on the edge of a big cling film sheet and fold over to seal in the spices; gently beat the chicken with a rolling pin until flattened to approximately 1 cm thick. Cook the chicken breasts for about 6 minutes each side on a griddle pan over medium heat, or until cooked through.
4. To make the salad, add all salad ingredients, except the avocado, in a large mixing bowl. Fold in the avocado slices gently and season with sea salt and black pepper.
5. Make the salsa: In a separate dish, mix all of the salsa ingredients; press the tomatoes with your hands until a chunky, juicy salsa forms.
6. Serve one chicken breast with a heaped spinach salad and mango salsa on the side.

Information Per **Makes:**

Calories: 182; Total Fat: 11.7 g; Carbs: 8.6 g; Dietary Fiber: 6.3 g; Protein: 19.3 g; Cholesterol: 65 mg; Sodium: 76 mg

---

125. *Healthy Black Bean Chili*

Tot time: 1 Hour 55 Minutes

Preparation time: 20 Minutes

Cooking Time: 1 hour 35 Minutes

Makes: 4-6

What you need:

- 1 tablespoon extra-virgin olive oil
- 1 red onion, finely chopped
- 3 cloves garlic, finely chopped
- 2 stalks celery, chopped
- 1 green bell pepper, chopped
- 2 red bell peppers, chopped
- 1 ½ cups chopped tomatoes

- Pinch of salt and pepper
- 1 ½ cups black beans
- 1 tablespoon cumin powder
- 2 teaspoons cinnamon powder
- 1 fresh red chili, deseeded and finely chopped
- 1 cup coconut milk
- 1 bunch fresh coriander, finely chopped
- Brown rice, to serve

Steps:

1. Heat extra virgin olive oil in a skillet set over medium heat until hot but not smoky; stir in red onion, garlic and celery until fragrant.
2. Stir in bell peppers and tomatoes, season with salt and pepper; cook for about 2 minutes, and then stir in the black beans. Cook for about 5 minutes and then stir in the spices and coconut milk. Simmer for a few minutes or until thick.
3. If desired, serve over a bed of steamed brown rice sprinkled with coriander and with sliced avocado on the side.

Per serving:

Calories: 358; Total Fat: 8.6 g; Net Carbs: 43.5 g; Dietary Fiber: 13.4g; Sugars: 6.2 g; Protein: 12.4 g; Cholesterol: 16 mg; Sodium: 30 mg

---

126.   Slow-Cooked Sweet Potato & Beef Curry

Tot time: 6 Hour 35 Minutes

Preparation time: 10 Minutes

Cooking Time: 6 Hour 15 Minutes

Makes: 8

What you need:

- 2 pounds beef chuck steak, trimmed, diced
- 1 pound sweet potato, peeled, diced
- 1 tablespoon extra-virgin olive oil
- 2 cups coconut milk
- 2 tablespoons Thai red curry paste
- 1 1/2 tablespoons curry sauce
- 3 kaffir lime leaves
- 1 lemongrass stem, bruised
- Fresh coriander leaves
- A pinch of salt and pepper

Steps:

1. Heat olive oil in a skillet set over medium-high heat and fry in beef for about 5 minutes or until browned; transfer to a slower cooker.
2. Add red onion, garlic, curry paste, and lemongrass to the skillet and cook for about 5 minutes or until fragrant; stir in coconut milk for about 2 minutes and then transfer the mixture to the slow cooker.
3. Add curry sauce to the pot and kaffir lime leaves and sweet potatoes and stir to mix. Cover the pot and cook on low for about 6 hours or until beef is very tender.
4. Stir the curry and remove kaffir lime leaves and lemongrass before serving. Serve topped with chopped coriander leaves.

Per serving:

Calories: 430; Total Fat: 25.25 g; Net Carbs: 15.1 g; Dietary Fiber: 3.5 g; Sugars: 5.7 g Protein: 31.9 g; Cholesterol: 71 mg; Sodium: 305 mg

---

127.   Coconut Steamed Brown Rice

Tot time: 35 Minutes

Preparation time: 5 Minutes

Cooking Time: 30 Minutes

Makes: 8

What you need:
- 3 cups coconut milk
- 1 teaspoon salt
- 2 tablespoons coconut oil
- 2 cups brown rice, rinsed

Steps:
1. In a saucepan, mix coconut milk, salt, and oil; bring to a gentle boil; add brown rice and stir to mix well.
2. Cover and simmer for about 25 minutes or until cooking liquid is absorbed and the rice is tender.
3. Remove from, stir and serve with favorite stew.

Per serving:

Calories: 260; Total Fat: 14 g; Net Carbs: 18.1 g; Dietary Fiber: 11 g; Sugar: 4 g; Protein: 3 g; Sodium: 291 mg; Cholesterol: 0 mg

---

128.   Grilled Pork & Black Bean Bowl

Tot time: 10 Minutes

Preparation time: 10 Minutes

Cooking Time: N/A

Makes: 6

What you need:

- 3/4 pound grilled pork roast, diced
- 2 cups cooked black beans, drained and rinsed
- 6 cups mixed salad greens
- 1/4 red onion, chopped
- 1/2 cup vinaigrette dressing

Steps:

1. Mix all ingredients in a large bowl; divide among serving plates, and serve right away.

Per serving:

Calories: 469; Total Fat: 29 g; Net Carbs: 48.1 g; Dietary Fiber: 12 g; Sugar: 19 g; Protein: 33 g; Sodium: 272 mg; Cholesterol: 49 mg

---

129.   Vegetable Stew

Preparation time: 10 Minutes

Cooking Time: 7 Hours

Servings: 12

What you need:

- 3 tsp garlic powder
- 2 medium onions, chopped
- 4 leek stalks, chopped
- 4 large carrots, sliced thick
- 2 small Acorn squash, seeded, peeled, and cut into 1 ½-inch chunk
- 1 (8-ounce) package sliced mushrooms
- 1 cup zucchini
- 1-pound small sweet potatoes
- 2 (15-ounce) can low sodium navy beans rinsed and drained
- 3 cup vegetable broth
- 2 (15-ounce) can tomatoes
- 2 bay leaves

Steps:

1. Place the garlic powder, onion, and all the vegetables in a 4–5- quart slow cooker.
2. Add the navy beans, vegetable broth, tomatoes, and bay leaf.
3. Simmer for 5 to 7 hours until the vegetables are tender.
4. Serve with crusty bread and Have a healthy meal!

Per serving:

Calories: 128; Total Fat: 1.2g; Cholesterol: 0mg; Sodium: 374 mg; Total Carbohydrate: 24.6g; Dietary Fiber: 6.4g; Total Sugars: 5.2g; Protein: 7.2g

---

130.   *Glazed Tempeh*

Preparation time: 5 Minutes

Cooking Time: 15 Minutes

Servings: 8

What you need:

- 2 pounds tempeh, trimmed
- 2 tbsp. coconut oil
- ½ cup apple cider vinegar
- 4 tbsp. maple syrup
- 2 tbsp. Dijon mustard

Steps:

1. Cut the tempeh into 1-inch slices. Using a medium-sized pan, heat the coconut oil until it begins to melt.
2. In the meantime, preheat the oven to 375 F and spray a baking sheet with non-stick cooking spray. Fry the tempeh for a minute on each side and place them on a baking sheet.
3. Whisk the vinegar, maple syrup, and Dijon mustard in a small bowl. Generously brush the tempeh with glaze. Bake for 10 minutes.

Per serving:

Calories: 280; Total Fat: 15.8g; Cholesterol: 0 mg; Sodium: 56 mg; Total Carbohydrate: 17.7g; Dietary Fiber: 0.1g; Total Sugars: 6g; Protein: 21.2g

Salad

131.   SKINNY CHICKEN SALAD

Tot time: 10 Minutes

Preparation time: 10 Minutes

Cooking Time: N/A

Makes: 4

What you need:

- 4 ounces shredded or diced (cooked) boneless, skinless, chicken breast (about 1 cup)
- 1/4 cup diced celery
- 2 tablespoons sliced green onion
- 1/4 cup diced sweet, crisp apple
- 1 tablespoon light mayo
- 1 tablespoon light sour cream or Greek yogurt
- optional: 1/2-1 Tablespoon chopped fresh parsley or cilantro
- 1/8 teaspoon curry powder
- 1/4 teaspoon red wine vinegar
- 1 tablespoon toasted sliced almonds
- salt and pepper to taste

Steps:

1. Mix all ingredients except almonds and stir to mix. If possible, chill for an hour or so before eating.
2. Before serving, mix in almonds.
3. Eat in a lettuce wrap, on whole grain bread, in a wrap, or in a pita.

Per serving:

Calories: 83.66; Total Fat: 5.24; Carbs: 2.31g; Cholesterol: 19mg; Sugars: 1g; Protein: 6.72g; Sodium: 259mg; Fiber: 0.71g

132.   Potato Salad

Tot time: 40 Minutes

Preparation time: 15 Minutes

Cooking Time: 25 Minutes

Makes: 4

What you need:

- 2 pounds tiny new potatoes
- 1 cup low-fat mayonnaise dressing or light salad dressing
- 2 stalks celery, chopped
- 1 large onion, chopped
- ⅓ cup chopped sweet or dill pickles
- ½ teaspoon salt
- ¼ teaspoon coarsely ground black pepper
- 2 hard-cooked eggs, chopped
- 1 to 2 tablespoons fat-free milk
- 1 Coarsely ground black pepper

Steps:

1. In a large saucepan, combine potatoes and enough water to cover potatoes. Bring to boiling; reduce heat. Cover and simmer for 15 to 20 minutes or just until tender. Drain well; cool potatoes. Cut potatoes into quarters.
2. In a large bowl, mix mayonnaise, celery, onion, pickles, salt and teaspoon pepper. Add the potatoes and egg, gently tossing to coat. Cover and chill for 6 to 24 hours.
3. To serve, stir enough of the milk into salad to reach the desired consistency. Season to taste with additional pepper.

Per serving:

Calories: 278.85; Total Fat: 4.11; Carbs: 53.44g; Cholesterol: 82mg; Sugars: 8.68g; Protein: 8.5g; Sodium: 779mg; Fiber: 5.8g

Soup

133.   Rice and Chicken Soup

Preparation time: 15 minutes

Cook time: 20 minutes

Makes: 6

What you need:

- 1 onion, diced small
- Olive or avocado oil
- 4 carrots, peeled and diced small
- Salt & Black pepper
- 3 celery ribs, diced small
- 1 teaspoon ground cumin
- 4 cloves garlic
- ½ teaspoon coriander
- Pinch cayenne pepper
- ½ teaspoon chili powder
- 5 cups warm chicken broth (or stock)
- 3 to 3 ½ cups cooked, shredded chicken
- ½ cup frozen peas, thawed
- ½ corn kernels
- 1 teaspoon lime zest
- 1 tablespoon lime juice
- Tortilla strips, Jalapeno slices, and lime wedges, for garnish
- 2 tablespoons of chopped cilantro, plus extra for serving
- 3 cups cooked rice

Steps:

1. Heat 4 tablespoons oil in a medium-large soup pot over medium-high heat; after the oil is heated, add the onion, carrots, and celery and sauté for 1-2 minutes.
2. Add a significant pinch of salt and black pepper to taste, as well as the cumin, coriander, chili powder, and sprinkle of cayenne pepper and sauté for a few more minutes, or until the vegetables, are soft.
3. Stir in the garlic and, until fragrant, add the chicken stock/broth.
4. Bring the soup to a boil, then lower to low heat, cover, and cook the veggies for 20 minutes or until tender.

5. Remove from the fire and toss in the shredded chicken, peas, corn kernels, lime zest, lime juice, and chopped cilantro; season with salt and pepper to taste.
6. To serve, spoon some of the rice (about 12 cups) into a bowl and ladle over the hot soup; garnish with extra lime, sliced jalapenos, or crunchy tortilla pieces.

Per serving:

Calories: 337; Total Fat: 12.86 g; Net Carbs: 38.15 g; Dietary Fiber: 2.6 g; Sugar: 4.9 g; Protein: 16.9 g; Sodium: 978 mg; Cholesterol: 750 mg

---

134.   Carrot Soup

Tot time: 1 Hour 20 Minutes

Preparation time: 20 Minutes

Cooking Time: 1 Hour

Makes: 6

What you need:
- 1 tbsp avocado oil
- 1 onion, peeled and chopped
- Salt and freshly ground black pepper
- 1-pound carrots, peeled and sliced
- 1 large sweet potato, peeled and diced
- 2 bay leaves
- 6 cups of chicken stock or vegetable stock, or water

Steps:
1. Heat the oil in a large saucepan over medium heat.
2. Add the onion and occasionally stir until tender but not golden, 8 to 10 minutes. Season with salt and pepper.
3. Add the carrot, sweet potato, bay leaves, and 5 cups of vegetable broth. Cover the pot. Cook 30 to 45 minutes until the vegetables are very tender.
4. Remove the bay leaves. Mix the soup in a mixer or food processor until very smooth. Add some of the remaining broth if the soup is too thick.
5. Season with salt and pepper. Serve hot.

Per serving:

Calories: 176; Total Fat: 5.36 g; Net Carbs: 25 g; Dietary Fiber: 3.4 g; Sugar:9.352 g; Protein: 7.5 g; Sodium: 541 mg; Cholesterol: 7.2 mg

---

135.   Carrot and Zucchini Soup

Tot time: 50 Minutes

Preparation time: 20 Minutes

Cooking Time: 30 minutes

Servings: 4

What you need:

- 1 tsp coconut oil
- 1 small onion, finely chopped
- ½ lb. carrots, peeled and sliced
- ½ lb. zucchini, unpeeled and sliced
- ½ cup pumpkin chopped
- ½ cup sweet potato diced
- 1 tsp curry powder
- 2 cups low-sodium vegetable broth,
- ⅛ cup fresh basil

Steps:

1. Sauté onions in a pot for 5 minutes or until just tender.
2. Add the carrots and zucchini, sweet potato and pumpkin, then the curry powder.
3. Stir for 1 to 2 minutes. Add the vegetable broth and bring to a boil.
4. Reduce the heat and simmer for 20 minutes. In the end, add the chopped basil.
5. Transfer the soup to a mixer and mix gently, working in two batches.
6. Serve and Have a healthy meal!

Per serving:

Calories: 100; Total Fat: 2.1g; Saturated Fat: 1.2g; Cholesterol: 0mg; Sodium: 438mg; Total Carbohydrate: 16.7g; Dietary Fiber: 3.6g; Sugars: 6.9g; Protein: 4.6g

---

136.   *Creamy Broccoli and Sweet Potato Soup*

Tot time: 55 Minutes

Preparation time: 20 Minutes

Cooking Time: 35 Minutes

Servings: 4

What you need:

- ½ tbsp coconut oil
- ½ onion, coarsely chopped
- 2 large cloves garlic, coarsely chopped
- 2 broccoli florets and stalks chopped

117

- 1 cauliflower florets
- 1 big sweet potato
- ¼ leek root, coarsely chopped
- 2 cups vegetable stock
- 2 cups coconut milk

Steps:

1. Heat the oil in a saucepan over medium heat.
2. Add the onion and garlic and cook and stir for 10 to 15 minutes until translucent.
3. Add the pilled and chopped sweet potatoes, broccoli florets, cauliflower florets, and leek. Stir until coated with oil. Top the vegetables with the vegetable broth and coconut milk; bring to a boil.
4. Reduce heat and simmer, occasionally stirring, until the vegetables can bite easily with a fork, 20 to 25 minutes. Remove the soup from the heat.
5. Don't fill a mixer more than half full with liquid and vegetables. Cover and hold the lid. Pulse several times before bringing the mixer to full speed.
6. Mix on fool speed for about a minute until the soup is creamy.
7. Repeat with the rest of the soup, working in batches.

Per serving:

Calories: 361; Total Fat: 30.6g; Cholesterol: 0mg; Sodium: 78mg; Total Carbohydrate: 22.1g; Dietary Fiber: 5.5g; Total Sugars: 8.7g; Protein: 5.7g

---

137.   *Fresh Kale Garlic Soup*

Tot time: 35 Minutes

Preparation time: 10 Minutes

Cooking Time: 25 Minutes

Servings: 8

What you need:

- 4 tsp coconut oil
- 2 medium sweet potatoes, peeled and cubed
- 1 medium onion, finely chopped
- 2 stalk leeks, finely chopped
- 2 tsp. garlic powder
- 2 cups vegetable broth
- 2 cups water
- 2 cups coconut milk
- 2 (6-ounce) bag baby kale, divided
- Freshly ground black pepper, to taste

- Kosher salt, to taste

Steps:

1. In a large saucepan or Dutch oven, heat the coconut oil.
2. Sauté the sweet potato, onion, leek, and garlic powder for 5 minutes.
3. Add the vegetable broth, water, and coconut milk. Bring to a boil and cover, then simmer for 10 minutes.
4. Add kale, cover, and simmer for another 10 minutes.
5. Let it slightly cool, then transfer to a mixer. If necessary, work in two batches to prevent hot soup from spilling into the mixer during mixing.
6. Season to taste and serve.

Per serving:

Calories: 235; Total Fat: 17.1g; Cholesterol: 0mg; Sodium: 255mg; Total Carbohydrate: 18.8g; Dietary Fiber: 3.7g; Total Sugars: 5.6g; Protein: 5g

---

138.   *Turkey and Orzo Soup*

Tot time: 2 Hours & 15 Minutes

Preparation time: 15 Minutes

Cooking Time: 2h

Servings: 5

What you need:

- 2-½ cups chicken broth
- 1 skinless, boneless turkey breast halves
- ½ cup diced leek
- ½ cup diced onion
- ⅛ cup diced carrots
- ⅛ cup green peas
- ¼ cup zucchini
- ¼ cup cauliflower
- ⅛ cup corn
- ⅛ cup drained and rinsed Kidney beans
- ½ tsp dried Rosemary
- ½ tsp ground black pepper
- ½ tsp salt
- 1 bay leaf
- ¾ cup orzo

Steps:

1. Bring the chicken broth to a boil in a pot. Cook the turkey breasts in boiling water until no longer pink in the center (about 20 minutes). Remove the turkey from the chicken broth using a slotted spoon and chop it with a fork.
2. Stir the grated turkey, leek, onion, carrots, green peas, corn, cauliflower, zucchini, kidney beans, rosemary, pepper, salt, and bay leaves in the chicken broth and cook until vegetables are cooked through - slightly tender and the flavors of the soup have mixd (about 20 minutes).
3. Add the orzo to the soup and simmer for about 30 min until the orzo is tender.

Per serving:

Calories: 173; Total Fat: 2.3g; Cholesterol: 13mg; Sodium: 557mg; Total Carbohydrate: 27.7g; Dietary Fiber: 2.6g; Total Sugars: 1.9g; Protein: 10.3g

---

139.   Couscous Salad

Tot time: 25 Minutes

Preparation time: 10 Minutes

Cooking Time: 15 Minutes

Servings: 4

What you need:

- ½ cup uncooked Couscous
- 1 cup fat-free, low-sodium vegetable broth
- ½ cup fresh green peas
- ½ cup chopped red pepper
- ½ 15-oz. can Kidney beans
- ½ cup grape tomatoes halved
- ⅛ cup finely chopped onion
- 1 Serrano pepper, finely chopped
- ⅛ cup chopped fresh basil
- Juice of 1 large lemon
- 1-½ tbsp. olive oil
- ¼ tsp cumin

Steps:

1. Rinse the Couscous well in a colander to remove the bitter layer.
2. Place the Couscous in a 2-liter saucepan with the vegetable broth. Bring to a boil, cover, and simmer for 10 to 15 minutes until the water is absorbed and the couscous is tender. Let cool.
3. Place the cooled cooked Couscous in a bowl with peas, red bell pepper, kidney beans, tomatoes, onions, Serrano, and basil.
4. Whisk together the lemon juice, olive oil, and cumin in a small bowl.

5. Drizzle and toss over the Couscous salad.

Per serving:

Calories: 164; Total Fat: 4g; Cholesterol: 0mg; Sodium: 200mg; Total Carbohydrate: 26.8g; Dietary Fiber: 4.2g; Total Sugars: 3.9g; Protein: 6g

---

140.   Pan-Seared Salmon Salad with Snow Peas & Grapefruit

Tot time: 15 Minutes

Preparation time: 15 Minutes

Cooking Time: N/A

Makes: 4

What you need:

- 4 (100g) skin-on salmon fillets
- 1/8 teaspoon sea salt
- 2 teaspoons extra virgin olive oil
- 4 cups arugula
- 8 leaves Boston lettuce, washed and dried
- 1 cup snow peas, cooked
- 2 avocados, diced

For Grapefruit-Dill Dressing:

- 1/4 cup grapefruit juice
- 1/4 cup extra virgin olive oil
- 1 teaspoon raw honey
- 1 tablespoon Dijon mustard
- 1 tablespoon chopped fresh dill
- 2 garlic cloves, minced
- 1/2 teaspoon salt

Steps:

1. Sprinkle fish with about 1/8 teaspoon salt and cook in 2 teaspoons of olive oil over medium heat for about 4 minutes per side or until golden. In a small bowl, whisk together all dressing ingredients and set aside.
2. Divide arugula and lettuce among four serving plates. Divide lettuce and arugula among 4 plates and add the remaining salad ingredients; top each with seared salmon and drizzle with dressing. Have a healthy meal!

Per serving:

Calories: 608; Total Fat: 46 g; Carbs: 16.2 g; Dietary Fiber: 8.7 g; Sugars: 5.1 g; Protein: 38.9 g; Cholesterol: 78 mg; Sodium: 488 mg

Tot time: 10 Minutes

Preparation time: 10 Minutes

Cooking Time: N/A

Makes: 4

What you need:

- 1 large avocado, sliced
- 1 red onion, thinly sliced
- 1 large fennel bulb, chopped
- 4 medium tomatoes, chopped
- 1 tablespoon avocado oil
- 3 tablespoons extra virgin olive oil
- 2 tablespoons fresh lime juice
- 2 tablespoons chopped fresh cilantro
- 1/8 teaspoon chili powder
- 1/8 teaspoon smoked paprika
- 1/8 teaspoon sea salt

Steps:

1. Mix avocado, red onion, fennel, and tomatoes in a bowl.
2. In a small bowl, whisk together avocado oil, extra virgin olive oil, lime juice, cilantro, chili powder, paprika, and salt; pour over the avocado mixture and toss to mix well. Have a healthy meal!

Per serving:

Calories: 231; Total Fat: 21 g; Carbs: 12 g; Dietary Fiber: 5.7 g; Sugars: 4.7 g; Protein: 2.4 g; Cholesterol: 0 mg; Sodium: 70 mg

142.   *Spiced Sweet Potato and Spring Onion Salad*

Tot time: 20 Minutes

Preparation time: 10 Minutes

Cooking Time: 10 Minutes

Makes: 4

What you need:

- 4 large sweet potatoes, peeled, diced

- 1 cup sliced spring onions
- 1 medium red bell pepper, chopped
- 2 tablespoons minced mint leaves
- 2 fresh minced chilies, chopped
- 1 tablespoon grated orange zest
- 2 teaspoons ground cumin
- ¼ cup apple cider vinegar
- 4 tablespoons extra-virgin olive oil
- ¼ teaspoon sea salt
- ¼ teaspoon black pepper

Directions

1. Preheat your oven to 350 degrees.
2. Place sweet potatoes on a baking sheet and drizzle with half of the oil; sprinkle with salt and pepper and toss to coat well. Bake in the preheated oven for about 30 minutes or until tender and browned.
3. Meanwhile, add the remaining oil to the mixer, bell pepper, vinegar, zest, cumin, sea salt, and pepper, and mix until very smooth.
4. Remove the potatoes from the oven and toss with chiles, mint, and spring onions. Drizzle with the dressing and toss to coat well. Have a healthy meal!

Per serving:

Calories: 325; Total Fat: 14.6 g; Net Carbs: 39.5 g; Dietary Fiber: 7.7 g; Sugars: 2.9; Protein: 3.4 g; Cholesterol: 0 mg; Sodium: 139 mg

---

143.   Low Carb Fruit Salad

Tot time: 10 Minutes

Preparation time: 10 Minutes

Cooking Time: 0 Minutes

Makes: 2

What you need:

- 1 cup mixed berries
- 3 tablespoons unsweetened Greek yogurt
- ½ tablespoon chia seeds
- ½ vanilla bean, scraped
- 1 sage leaf, cut into small pieces

Steps:

1. Add the berries to a large bowl and mix in the chopped sage. In a small bowl, mix the Greek yogurt, chia seeds, and scraped vanilla until well mixed, then set aside for 5 minutes.
2. Add the yogurt mixture to the berries and mix well. Chill in the fridge before serving.
3. Have a healthy meal!

Nutrition info Per **Makes:**

Calories: 151; Total Fat: 2.3 g; Net Carbs: 6 g; Dietary Fiber: 4g; Sugars: 0.8; Protein: 8 g; Cholesterol: 0 mg; Sodium: 10 mg

---

144. *Fat Flush & Detox Salad*

Tot time: 10 Minutes

Preparation time: 10 Minutes

Cooking Time: N/A

Makes: 6

What you need:

For the salad:

- 2 cups broccoli florets
- 2 cups red cabbage, thinly sliced
- 2 cups chopped kale
- 1 cup grated carrot
- 1 red bell pepper, sliced into strips
- 2 avocados, diced
- 1/2 cup chopped parsley
- 1 cup walnuts
- 1 tablespoon sesame seeds

For the dressing:

- 2 teaspoons gluten-free mustard
- 1 tablespoon freshly grated ginger
- 1/2 cup fresh lemon juice
- 1/3 cup grapeseed oil
- 1 teaspoon raw honey
- 1/4 teaspoon salt

Steps:

1. In a mixer, mix all the dressing ingredients until well mixed; set aside. In a salad bowl, mix broccoli, cabbage, kale, carrots, and bell pepper; pour the dressing over the salad and toss until well coated. Add diced avocado, parsley, walnuts, and sesame seed; toss again to coat and serve.

Per serving:

Calories: 437; Total Fat: 38.7 g; Carbs: 19.6 g; Dietary Fiber: 8.9 g; Sugars: 5.2 g; Protein: 9.1 g; Cholesterol: 0 mg; Sodium: 153 mg

---

145.   *Ultimate Slimming & Detox Soup*

Tot time: 35 Minutes

Preparation time: 15 Minutes

Cooking Time: 20 Minutes

Makes: 6

What you need:

- 2 tablespoons extra-virgin olive oil
- 1 cup chopped shallot
- 1 tablespoon grated ginger
- 2 cloves garlic, minced
- 4 cups homemade chicken broth
- 1 medium golden beet, diced
- 1 large carrot, sliced
- 1 cup shredded red cabbage
- 1 cup sliced mushrooms
- a handful of pea pods, halved
- 1 hot chili pepper, sliced
- 1 cup chopped cauliflower
- 1 cup chopped broccoli
- 1 bell pepper, diced
- A pinch of cayenne pepper
- A pinch of sea salt
- 1 cup baby spinach
- 1 cup chopped kale
- 1 cup grape tomatoes, halved

Steps:

1. In a large skillet, heat olive oil until hot but not smoky; sauté in shallots, ginger, and garlic for about 2 minutes or until tender; stir in broth and bring the mixture to a gentle simmer.
2. Add in beets and carrots and simmer for about 5 minutes. Stir in hot pepper, cauliflower, and broccoli and cook for about 3 minutes. Stir in bell pepper, red cabbage, mushrooms, and peas and cook for 1 minute.
3. Remove from heat and stir in salt and pepper. Stir in leafy greens and tomatoes and cover the pot for about 5 minutes. Serve.

Per serving:

Calories: 111.64; Total Fat: 5.6 g; Carbs: 13.36 g; Dietary Fiber: 3.69 g; Sugars: 6.69 g; Protein: 4.6 g; Cholesterol: 3.2 mg; Sodium: 653.7 mg

---

146.   *Delicious Squash Soup*

Tot time: 40 Minutes

Preparation time: 10 Minutes

Cooking Time: 30 Minutes

Makes: 4

What you need:

- 2 tablespoons coconut oil
- 1 cup chopped red onions
- 1 cup chopped leek
- 2 carrots, diced
- 1 tablespoon minced ginger
- 4 cloves garlic
- 2 cups diced butternut squash
- 1 tablespoon Thai green curry paste
- 2 cups homemade chicken stock
- 1 cup coconut milk

Steps:

1. Heat coconut oil in a large skillet; stir in red onions, leeks, and carrots and sauté for about 5 minutes or until tender. Stir in curry paste and add garlic, ginger, and squash. Cook for about 3 minutes and then stir in chicken stock.
2. Simmer for about 20 minutes and then stir in coconut milk. Cook for a few minutes and then transfer to a food processor.
3. Pulse until the soup is smooth. Serve hot!

Per serving:

Calories: 310; Total Fat: 23 g; Carbs: 22.8 g; Dietary Fiber: 4 g; Sugars: 8.59 g; Protein: 6.3 g; Cholesterol: 4.3 mg; Sodium: 403 mg

---

147.   *Warm Bean Soup with Whole-Wheat Tortilla Chips*

Tot time: 1 Hour 10 Minutes

Preparation time: 10 Minutes

Cooking Time: 1 Hour

Makes: 6

What you need:

- 6 cups boiling water
- 1 large red onion, diced
- 1 pound dried black beans
- 1/4 teaspoon chipotle chile powder
- 2 teaspoons cumin
- 1 teaspoon sea salt
- 1 cup salsa
- 12 ounces frozen corn kernels
- 1 tablespoon fresh lime juice
- Avocado slices
- baked Whole-wheat tortilla chips

Steps:

1. Boil water in an instant pot and turn it to sauté setting; add onion and cook, often stirring, until tender and browned.
2. Stir in beans, chipotle chili powder, cumin, boiling water, and sea salt; turn off the sauté function. Lock lid in place and turn on high pressure, adjusting time to 30 minutes. Let the pressure come down naturally before opening the pot.
3. Remove about 3 cups of beans to a mixer and mix until very smooth; return to pot and add salsa and corn. Adjust seasoning and turn the pot on sauté; cook until heated through.
4. Ladle in serving bowls and drizzle with lime juice, garnish with avocado slices, and serve with baked tortilla chips.

Per serving:

Calories: 329; Total Fat: 1 g; Carbs: 65 g; Dietary Fiber: 15 g; Sugars: 7 g; Protein: 18 g; Cholesterol: 0 mg; Sodium: 707 mg

---

148.   Creamy Chicken and Farro Soup

Tot time: 70 Minutes

Preparation time: 10 Minutes

Cooking Time: 60 Minutes

Makes: 6

What you need:

- 3 cups cooked and shredded chicken
- ¾ cups dry farro
- ¼ cup almond flour
- 4 cups chicken stock
- 1 ½ cups milk
- 1 tablespoon extra-virgin olive oil

- ¼ cup unsalted butter
- 1 red onion, diced
- 2 garlic cloves, minced
- 1 large carrot, diced
- 2 celery ribs, diced
- 2 teaspoons minced sage
- 1 tablespoon minced thyme
- salt and pepper to taste

Steps:

1. Heat oil in a large oil set over medium-high heat; stir in farro and toast for about 1 minute; stir in salt, pepper, and stock and then bring a gentle boil. Lower the heat and simmer for about 20 minutes.
2. Meanwhile, melt butter in a large skillet and cook red onion, garlic, carrots, celery, salt, and pepper for about 5 minutes. Stir in sage and thyme for about 1 minute and then stir in flour for about 2 minutes; whisk in milk and simmer for about 4 minutes or until the mixture is thick; pour into the farro and stir in chicken, salt, and pepper.
3. Cook for about 25 minutes or until farro is cooked through.

Per serving:

Calories: 410; Total Fat: 17.1 g; Net Carbs: 26.8 g; Dietary Fiber: 6.4 g; Sugars: 4.8 g Protein: 29g; Cholesterol: 79 mg; Sodium: 658 mg

---

149.   *Lentil Super Salad*

Tot time: 10 Minutes

Preparation time: 10 Minutes

Cooking Time: N/A

Makes: 4

What you need:

- ¼ cup chicory leaves
- ¼ cup chopped celery leaves
- 2 tablespoons sliced red onion
- 1 tablespoon extra-virgin olive oil
- 1 large Medjool date, chopped
- 1 tablespoon capers
- ¼ cup rocket
- 2 avocados, peeled, stoned, and sliced
- ½ cup lentils

- 2 tablespoon chopped walnuts
- 1 tablespoon fresh lemon juice
- ¼ cup chopped parsley

Steps:

1. Arrange salad leaves in a large bowl or a plate; mix the remaining ingredients well and serve over the salad leaves.

Per serving:

Calories: 359; Total Fat: 25.8 g; Carbs: 26.8g; Dietary Fiber: 15.2g; Protein: 9.7g; Cholesterol: 0mg; Sodium: 80mg

---

150. Chickpea Salad Wrap

Tot time: 5 Minutes

Preparation time: 5 Minutes

Cooking Time: N/A

Makes: 3

What you need:

- 1 ½ cups cooked chickpeas
- 1/4 cup toasted sunflower seeds
- 1 tablespoon minced fresh dill
- 3 tablespoons chopped dill pickle
- 2 tablespoons chopped red onion
- 1/2 cup chopped celery
- 2 tablespoons fresh lemon juice
- 1/2 tsp regular mustard
- 1 garlic clove, minced
- ¼ teaspoon sea salt
- ¼ teaspoon pepper
- Whole wheat tortillas

Steps:

1. In a large bowl, mix all the ingredients, mashing the chickpeas until smooth. Stuff the mixture into a wrap and serve.

Per serving:

Calories: 302 Total Fat: 6.3 g; Carbs: 48.2 g; Dietary Fiber: 14 g; Sugars: 8.8 g; Protein: 15.6 g; Cholesterol: 0 mg; Sodium: 237 mg

---

151. Healthy Quinoa & Beef Salad

Tot time: 20 Minutes

Preparation time: 10 Minutes

Cooking Time: 10 Minutes

Makes: 6

What you need:

- 4 (150g) roast beef
- 3 cups cooked quinoa
- 1/2 red onion, thinly sliced
- 1 cup halved cherry tomatoes
- 1 cup baby spinach
- 1 cup rocket leaves
- 1 tablespoon chopped parsley
- 1 cup balsamic dressing

Steps:

1. In a large bowl, mix together cooked quinoa, onion, tomato, rocket, spinach, and parsley; divide among salad bowls and season with salt and pepper; top with roast beef and drizzle with dressing.
2. Have a healthy meal!

Per serving:

Calories: 332; Total Fat: 8.4 g; Net Carbs: 26.7 g; Dietary Fiber: 4.2 g; Sugars: 0.6 g
Protein: 32.2g; Cholesterol: 76 mg; Sodium: 73 mg

---

152.   *Shaved Veggie Salad with Toasted Pumpkin Seeds*

Tot time: 5 Minutes

Preparation time: 5 Minutes

Cooking Time: N/A

Makes: 2

What you need:

- 4 ounces spinach
- 2 watermelon radishes, thinly sliced
- 1 small yellow squash, thinly sliced
- 1 small yellow or red beet, thinly sliced
- 1 small cucumber, thinly sliced
- 1 small carrot, thinly sliced
- 1 tablespoon toasted pumpkin seeds
- 1 tablespoon extra-virgin olive oil

- 1 lemon, juiced
- sea salt, to taste ground pepper, to taste

Steps:

1. Mix veggies in a large bowl and toss with lemon juice and olive oil; season with salt and pepper and serve right away.

Per serving:

Calories: 159; Total Fat: 9.6 g; Carbs: 17.3 g; Dietary Fiber: 4.4 g; Sugars: 8.6 g; Protein: 5.4 g; Cholesterol: 0 mg; Sodium: 225 mg

---

153. Delicious Farro Salad with Italian Dressing

Tot time: 45 Minutes

Preparation time: 15 Minutes

Cooking Time: 30 Minutes

Makes: 8

What you need:

Salad:

- 1 cup uncooked Farro
- 1/4 teaspoon sea salt
- 1/2 cup sundried tomatoes
- 1 cup frozen peas
- 2 cups cherry tomatoes, halved
- 3/4 cup jarred roasted red peppers, drained, diced
- 1 large cucumber, diced
- 1/2 cup finely chopped fresh parsley

Italian Dressing:

- 1/4 cup fresh lemon juice
- 1/4 cup extra-virgin olive oil
- 1 tablespoon raw honey
- 1 teaspoon dried oregano
- 2 teaspoons Dijon mustard
- 1/2 teaspoon sea salt
- 1/4 teaspoon ground black pepper

Steps:

1. Rinse farro and drain; follow package instructions to cook until cooked through; transfer to a large bowl.

2. Meanwhile, in a small bowl, mix together olive oil, raw honey, mustard, fresh lemon juice, oregano, salt, and pepper until well mixd; pour half of the dressing over the warm farro. Sprinkle with sea salt and toss to coat well.
3. Add the remaining ingredients into the farro bowl and toss to mix well. Serve right away.

Per serving:

Calories: 186; Total Fat: 8.2g; Carbs: 26.11g; Dietary Fiber: 3.77g; Protein: 4.7g; Cholesterol: 0mg; Sodium: 225.78mg; Sugars: 7g

---

154.   Red Lentil and Chickpea Soup

Tot time: 50 Minutes

Preparation time: 20 Minutes

Cooking Time: 30 Minutes

Servings: 4

What you need:

- 1 tsp coconut oil
- 1 cup finely chopped onion
- 1 small leek stalk, diced
- 1 tsp garlic powder
- ½ tbsp ground cumin
- ½ tbsp paprika
- ½ cup rinsed red lentils
- 1 (15-ounce) cans reduced-sodium chickpeas, drained and rinsed
- ½ (14.5-ounce) can diced tomatoes
- 1 cup fat-free, low-sodium vegetable broth
- 1 cup water

Steps:

1. Heat the coconut oil in a saucepan over medium heat.
2. Fry the onions, leek, and garlic powder for about 4 to 5 minutes, until just tender.
3. Sprinkle with cumin and paprika and cook for 1 minute until fragrant.
4. Add the red lentils, chickpeas, tomatoes, water, and broth.
5. Bring to a boil and cover. Simmer for around 25 minutes or until lentils are tender.
6. Serve and Have a healthy meal!

Per serving:

Calories: 234; Total Fat: 2.6 g; Net Carbs: 41 g; Dietary Fiber: 9.1 g; Sugar: 8.5 g; Protein: 12.7 g; Sodium: 341 mg; Cholesterol: 0 mg

---

155.   Coconut-Black Bean Soup

Tot time: 40 Minutes

Preparation time: 10 Minutes

Cooking Time: 30 Minutes

Makes: 6

What you need:

- 4 cups canned black beans, drained, rinsed
- 2 cups diced tomatoes
- 2 cups coconut milk
- 1 cup vegetable broth
- 1 cup chopped green onions
- 2 cloves garlic, minced
- 1 tablespoon ground turmeric
- 1 tablespoon ground cumin
- 1 tablespoon ground ginger
- 1 pinch salt

Steps:

7. In a saucepan, mix together all the ingredients and bring to a gentle boil. Lower heat and simmer, covered, for about 30 minutes.
8. Remove from heat and serve hot over cooked rice or as is.

Per serving:

Calories: 336; Total Fat: 22 g; Net Carbs: 4.6 g; Dietary Fiber: 16 g; Sugar: 2 g; Protein: 15 g; Sodium: 998 mg; Cholesterol: 0 mg

CONCLUSION

I hope you enjoyed creating the amazing cocktail recipes included in this book!

As we have seen in the introduction, the gallbladder diet is NOT a curative nutritional regimen, but preventive. This is because solid crystals, once formed in the gallbladder, are totally insoluble and therefore irreversible with the simple dietary intervention.

The role of diet in the occurrence and prevention, both primary and secondary, of gallstones and bile duct stones is often overlooked, due to the many risk factors involved in the origin of this pathology.

On the other hand, most of the diseases have a multifactorial origin and this explains why some people - despite following a rather unhealthy diet at high risk for the development of certain diseases - never suffer from these diseases, and vice versa.

However, data in hand, there is no doubt that some dietary habits and particular lifestyles play, more than others, a major role in the etiopathogenesis of some diseases.

One of the most important factors leading to gallstone formation is the supersaturation of cholesterol in bile, resulting in lipid precipitation.

Such precipitation can occur either because of excess cholesterol itself, or because of deficiency of substances that keep it in solution (such as phospholipids and bile salts).

Another predisposing factor is prolonged dehydration, which concentrates the bile and emphasizes the supersaturation mentioned above.

Insufficient emptying of the gallbladder or too long periods between one emptying and another can also favor the separation-precipitation of bile components.

Role of sugars and insulin

It is hypothesized that the high intake of dietary sugars, besides predisposing to obesity, increases the synthesis of cholesterol as a consequence of the increased insulin stimulus.

Also the specific supplementation of vitamin C would seem to be useful in preventive terms.

Of course, as with all the evidence presented in this article, the conditional is a must. In fact, many other factors come into play in the onset of gallstones, such as genetic predisposition, diabetes, and the assumption of certain estrogen-based drugs (menopausal replacement therapy and birth control pills), which increase the concentration of cholesterol in the gallbladder and reduce its contractility.

Put this cookbook to good use. When you want to eat healthily and prevent diseases, just flip trough this book and pick your favorite dish... Have a healty meal!

Made in United States
North Haven, CT
02 May 2023

36130998R00076